Inadmissible to Canada

Travel to Canada After a Conviction

Second Edition

Marisa Feil

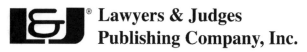

® Lawyers & Judges
Publishing Company, Inc.

Tucson, Arizona

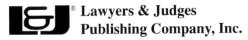

**Lawyers & Judges
Publishing Company, Inc.**

P.O. Box 30040 • Tucson, AZ 85751-0040
(520) 323-1500 • FAX (520) 323-0055
e-mail: sales@lawyersandjudges.com
www.lawyersandjudges.com

Library of Congress Cataloging-in-Publication Data

Names: Feil, Marisa, author.
Title: Inadmissible to Canada : travel to Canada after a conviction / Marisa
  Feil.
Description: Second edition. | Tucson, Arizona : Lawyers & Judges Publishing
  Company, Inc., [2019] | Includes bibliographical references and index.
Identifiers: LCCN 2018061478| ISBN 9781936360741 (softcover : alk. paper) |
  ISBN 1936360748 (softcover : alk. paper)
Subjects: LCSH: Emigration and immigration law--Canada. | Travel
  restrictions--Canada. | Alien criminals--Canada. | Criminal
  records--Canada.
Classification: LCC KE4454 .F45 2019 | DDC 342.7108/2--dc23
LC record available at https://lccn.loc.gov/2018061478

ISBN 13: 978-1-936360-74-1
ISBN 10: 1-936360-74-8

Printed in the United States of America
10 9 8 7 6 5 4 3 2 1

Contents

Acknowledgments

I would like to extend my gratitude and acknowledge the hard work of

Daisy Mellar

on the update of this book. I could not have completed this without you.

Dedication

I would like to acknowledge and thank the contributions of my staff, and the support of my family and friends. I am thankful and humbled by all of their support and love.

Foreword

It is no secret that criminality affects all facets of life and touches all of us, regardless of status or occupation.

Just imagine, you are fourth in the inspection line at Toronto International Airport's "Visitor Arrivals," patiently awaiting inspection by a Canada Border Services Agent (CBSA), when you begin to take inventory of the day's events. The flight from Kansas City was uneventful, but you are filled with nervous energy in anticipation of tomorrow's 9:00 a.m. business meeting. You are scheduled to make a presentation on behalf of your employer, a publicly-traded mergers and acquisition entity based in the United States. You recall that your exponential rise within the company's executive tier was due, in large part, to your post-graduate education and outstanding performance reviews. The company's Chief Operating and Financial Officers, with whom you are traveling, deem tomorrow's meeting with a well-known Canadian firm as the potential "deal of a lifetime."

Finally, you are summoned by the CBSA officer and within a few minutes are asked, "Have you ever been charged with an offence or convicted of a crime?"

The officer's inquiry rings loudly in your ears, evoking memories of early morning bells on the Kansas State University campus, where you had been charged and convicted years ago of *Driving While Impaired*. The CBSA officer advises you that, as a consequence of your conviction, you are member of an inadmissible class of persons found described in A36(2)(b) of the *Immigration and Refugee Protection Act* and are prohibited from entering Canada. An overwhelming and maddening rush of embarrassment consumes your every thought. You are left asking yourself, "If I can't enter Canada, what impact will this have on my future with the company?" So follow the questions, "What now?" and "Who can help me?"

Beyond the stigma of a conviction, few non-residents realize that their criminal history can result in the loss of visiting privileges to Canada. Luckily, short and long-term solutions exist through applications for a Temporary Resident Permit and Criminal Rehabilitation.

The above scenario is one to which author of *Inadmissible to Canada*, Marisa Feil can all too readily attest. In her experience with cases of criminal inadmissibility, Ms. Feil has faced clients asking her to do the impossible - provide immediate remedies to their unique situations and render submissions that will produce a successful outcome. In dealing with clients, Marisa strikes a healthy balance between offering expert advice and managing their expectations. No one comprehends the general principles of transparency, procedural fairness, and reasonableness more than Ms. Feil, when she submits applications to Canada Immigration for consideration. As a former Designated Immigration Officer with the Canadian Consulate General in Buffalo, I reviewed Marisa's submissions for Temporary Resident Permits and Applications for Criminal Rehabilitation, all of which she had expertly prepared. On the basis of her thorough submissions, I routinely recommended their acceptance, and the Minister's Delegate consistently concurred.

Drawing from her extensive knowledge and expertise in these areas, Marisa Feil has prepared a concise guide for legal practitioners like herself with clients possessing criminal records and seeking entry to Canada. With the use of this guide legal advocates may better navigate through the immigration admissibility process. In turn, advocates may better prepare their clients, so that - unlike the previously described business visitor – transgressions of the past do not close the door to opportunities of the future.

—Mary M. Keefe, (ret.) Designated Immigration Officer

Preface

When I was a young law student, I showed up on my first day of work at a Canadian immigration law firm and my boss, an extremely well respected immigration attorney, told me I would be working immigration cases for individuals who had been convicted of crimes outside of Canada. I could not have been more surprised. I was surprised for several reasons, the first of which was that my only exposure to criminal law was two classes I took in law school and an unthinkable number of hours watching crime & detective shows on television. I never thought that a person with a criminal record would even attempt to immigrate to another country. I didn't think it was possible and I certainly didn't think there was a way to overcome something like a previous conviction. With my limited understanding, I also could not understand how it was in Canada's interest to admit individuals who had convictions to this country.

The moment I worked on my first case, I understood. It was a spousal sponsorship case: a Canadian man had fallen in love with an American woman who had a Driving Under the Influence (DUI) conviction seven years before. My job was to put together her application for Criminal Rehabilitation so that her application to be sponsored by her husband would be approved. She was based in the U.S. and her husband in Canada and she was unable to travel to Canada because of her conviction. At that moment, it all clicked. When I thought of criminal convictions, a DUI was not the first that came to mind. I was shocked to find that something as seemingly minor as a DUI could prevent entry in to Canada.

A few months into the job, I received a handwritten letter from an 80-year-old man in New Jersey. He had written a beautiful letter about how his dream, before he passed away, was to take his youngest grandson on a fishing trip in Canada so that the boy could see Niagara Falls. He had been convicted of Fraud in the amount of 10 million dollars, more than 20 years before. I never thought I would have compassion for someone who committed such a serious offence until I learned his story. He had been running a family business that supported his brothers and their children and it had not been doing well. He had falsified orders and submitted these to the bank in order to receive a larger line of credit. He ended up turning himself in because he could not live with the guilt of what he had done. He asked for my help so that he could travel to Canada just one time, with his grandson. At that moment, I realized that there were probably millions of individuals who were good people, who were no danger to Canadians, and who didn't deserve to have their past prevent them from traveling to this great country.

That man's application was approved and is one I will definitely never forget. His case was processed in a new department at the firm I was working at as a law student and young lawyer. We assisted individuals who were immigrating to or simply traveling to Canada after criminal convictions. This went on to become the area of law that I would specialize in and it became the basis for my own practice, as well as the subject of many webinars, seminars and now this book.

This book is a hybrid of immigration law and criminal law, and is intended for criminal lawyers and judges located outside of Canada who represent clients who may have some need to travel to Canada. This book provides practical advice for representing clients domestically and can serve as a guide to help advise clients who are facing pending charges, trials, and sentencing hearings. Failure to have access to this information may result in significant hardship for clients who seek admittance to Canada following a conviction.

Every webinar, seminar, and piece of advice I give always comes with the preface that the information I share is practical in nature. I represent hundreds of clients crossing the Canadian border each year, for various different reasons. I have included all of the relevant legislation, operational guides, and jurisprudence in the text but most importantly, I have shared my experience over several years and thousands of clients so that clients can receive the best advice and representation possible from their attorneys.

Chapter 1

The Evolution of Criminal Inadmissibility in Canada

1.1 History

Canada has a complex history of ever-evolving immigration policies premised on balancing the dual priorities of ensuring public safety and welcoming newcomers. In the 19th and early 20th centuries, Canada's immigration policies focused on population growth, with the encouragement and incentivization of European immigration to develop and populate both rural and urban areas. This was followed by a shift in the latter part of the 20th century to an economic-based process that favored high-skilled, high-earning migrants. Canada's present-day immigration policy is even more selective, economically driven, and public safety-oriented under the current *Immigration and Refugee Protection Act* (hereafter *IRPA*).[1]

---

1.   Ninette Kelley & MJ Trebilcock, *The Making of the Mosaic: a history of Canadian immigration policy* (Toronto: University of Toronto Press, 1998) [Kelley].

Understanding the evolution of Canada's dynamic immigration policies requires a step-by-step review of the various acts and regulations that have been in effect within the past 15 decades.

A. The 1869 *Act Respecting Immigration and Immigrants*

In 1869, the *Act Respecting Immigration and Immigrants* (hereafter *ARII*) was created with the explicit purposes to promote population growth, define different immigrant categories, set about procedural rules, and deter the spread of diseases.[2] This focus on populating Canada led to minimal immigration barriers, so there was no concrete concept of criminal inadmissibility at the time. The *ARII* goes on to explain the few immigration barriers that it did have, including the right to refuse pauper immigrants, the very poor and destitute, and the right to force shipmasters to pay very high prices for anybody that brought over that was a "lunatic, idiotic, deaf and dumb, blind or infirm person not belonging to any Immigrant family."[3] Therefore, in 1869 there existed medical inadmissibility, albeit there was no system in place to formally declare who was considered any of the aforementioned categories, and a class-related inadmissibility. Alongside these immigration barriers, the *Immigration Act 1869* did provide some rights for immigrants, including rules of where they must be dropped off and at what time, and their right to remain on board or keep luggage on the ship for at least 48 hours after arrival.[4] Section 22 also dictated that lodgings in areas where immigrants are entering must provide lists of all the local rates so that they can make informed decisions, with penalties for non-complying hotels or inns.[5]

B. 1872 *Act to Amend the Immigration Act of 1869*

In 1872, there were 17 amendments to the *1869 Immigration Act*, of which two are of particular importance. Section 11 of the *Act to Amend the Immigration Act of 1869*, dictated that anybody employed on a vessel could not seduce a female immigrant "under promise of marriage, or by threats, or by the exercise of his authority, or by solicitation, or the making of gifts or presents."[6] This amendment is important because it both protected women from being taken advantage of whilst isolated on board a vessel, and improved the likelihood of women immigrating to Canada without a family, something the population needed since there was a gross gender imbalance at the time. Section 12 of the 1872 Amendment went so far as to prohibit employed men from letting women into their rooms, or going into the female immigrants rooms, without the captain's permission.[7]

2. *An Act Respecting Immigration and Immigrants*, Canada 1869, c 10.
3. *Ibid* at s 16; *Ibid* at s 11 (2).
4. *Ibid* at s 19(2); *Ibid* at s 17.
5. *Ibid.*
6. *An Act to Amend the Immigration Act of 1869*, Canada 1872, c 28 s 11.
7. *Ibid* at s 12.

Most importantly however, is Section 10 of the *Act to Amend the Immigration Act of 1869*, as it is the origin of criminal inadmissibility in Canada. This section gave the Governor in Council the ability to prohibit the landing of any criminal, or any other vicious class of immigrant from entering the country.[8] Consequently, the origins of criminal inadmissibility are to bar entry on the command of one person, without a normalized procedure or application process, and without a Board to oversee the otherwise indiscriminate commands of the Governor. Since there was only one person to make such distinctions of inadmissibility, the scope of said inadmissibility would have been rather small, as there was no way the Governor could go through, or even have enough background information on, each passenger.

C. *The Immigration Act of 1906*

In stark contrast to the relatively open door policies of the 19th Century, *The Immigration Act, 1906*, starts off the 20th Century by imposing new immigration barriers, head taxes, and a minimum net worth requirement that applied to specific classes of immigrants.[9] Another important aspect of this Act was that it created a legislative framework for deporting individuals that the government deemed inadmissible. One such category was the vastly expanding concept of medical inadmissibility, which changed drastically from 1869 to 1906. In 1906, the Act called for medical inspections of all passengers in suitable facilities, which meant that each passenger had to pass their health examination in order to be admitted.[10] *The Immigration Act, 1906*, had an entire list of prohibited immigrants, which included the insane and epileptic, those afflicted with a loathsome or contagious disease that could be a danger to public health, paupers and beggars, criminals, and prostitutes.[11] What is interesting here for the evolution of criminal inadmissibility is that this Act defines criminal inadmissibility as those crimes involving moral turpitude; "conduct that is contrary to justice, honesty or morality."[12] Furthermore, criminal inadmissibility went from being judged by the Governor alone, to having immigration agents that could make judgment calls on their own, which is far more similar to the contemporary system.[13] The introduction of agents that make inadmissibility calls for the Governor vastly expanded the scope of criminal inadmissibility.

---

8. *Ibid* at s 10.
9. *An Act Respecting Immigration and Immigrants*, Canada 1906, c 19. [Immigration Act 1906].
10. *Ibid* at s 22–23.
11. *Ibid* at s 26–29.
12. Bryan A. Garner, *Black's Law Dictionary*, 8th ed (St. Paul: Thomson West, 2004) at 1030. [Garner].
13. *Supra* Immigration Act 1906 at s 3.

D. *The Immigration Act of 1910*

An Act respecting Immigration, 1910, expanded the Governor's power to make indiscriminate judgments in terms of admissibility and deportation, created the idea of permanent residency (after three years), and expanded the list of prohibited immigrants deemed inadmissible.[14] Prohibited Classes in 1910 included: persons mentally defective (idiots, imbeciles, feeble-minded, epileptics, insane people, and people who had been insane within five years previously), diseased persons, persons physically defective (dumb, blind, or otherwise), criminals, prostitutes and pimps, procurers of prostitutes, beggars and vagrants, charity immigrants, and persons not complying with regulations.[15] The prohibition on the diseased and mentally defective was especially harsh, as there was no right to appeal if a medical officer had deemed them inadmissible and ordered them deported.[16]

Another noteworthy aspect of this Act is Section 37, which differentiates the minimum amount of money that immigrants and tourists' alike need to have in their possession to be admissible based on their race, occupation, or destination.[17] This gave the Canadian government an immigration control mechanism, as they could alter the minimum net worth for each race and occupation at any time in order to receive those they wanted and deter 'undesirables', an overt mechanism of discrimination. Furthermore, this control mechanism could channel immigrant flows to particular areas by making less desirable areas much cheaper. Section 40 and Section 42(2) are also pertinent to the development of criminal inadmissibility, as they stated that "any person... within three years after landing in Canada [that has been] convicted of a criminal offence in Canada" can be "deported forthwith, as provided for in section 33 of this Act... with right of appeal."[18] This is an important distinction, as it creates an extended timeline for the applicability of inadmissibility from the moment immigrants land to three years after they had arrived. Therefore, the *1910 Immigration Act* extended the timeline of the applicability of criminal inadmissibility, created the permanent resident immigration track, extended the prohibited categories, controlled immigration flows by race and occupation, and extended the absolute powers of the Governor.

E. Fairclough's 1962 Immigration Regulations

Following the introduction of the 1960 Bill of Rights and the Holocaust/Second World War, came a period of increased sensitivity to racial discrimination.[19] El-

---

14. *An Act respecting Immigration*, Canada 1910, c 27.
15. *Ibid* at s 3.
16. *Ibid* at s 18.
17. *Ibid.*
18. *Ibid.*
19. "Immigration Regulations, Order-in-Council PC 1962-68, 1962", online: Canadian Museum of Immigration at Pier 21 < http://www.pier21.ca/research/immigration-history/im-

len Fairclough, Minister of Citizenship and Immigration in 1962, took notice of this increased sensitivity and replaced the *1910 Immigration Act*'s control mechanism, which used ethnicity and occupation as determining factors, with one that used an immigrant's skills as the main criteria for determining admissibility.[20] Though Fairclough challenged overt racial discrimination within immigration regulations and legislation, covert racial discrimination persisted.[21] With Fairclough's changes, unsponsored immigrants could come in regardless of their color, race, or national origin, as long as they had a specific job waiting for them, could support themselves, were not criminals or terrorists, and did not have a disease that could threaten public health.[22] This meant that criminal and medical inadmissibility were further developed, but that overall, overt discrimination decreased. In Section 28(1), the 1962 Regulations required that immigrants have an immigration visa with them upon entering in order to be admissible to Canada; thus, instead of open doors, there was now an application process, and a queue, to undergo prior to migration.[23] Section 29(1) goes on to explain medical inadmissibility and the requirement that all passports and visas needed to have a medical certificate signed by a medical officer to enter.[24] This idea of having the proper visas and certificates prior to arrival made a huge difference in the application process, as it was completely different from the "show up and find out" mentality of the 19th century, where people had to find out at the border and uncertainty was rampant.

F. Prime Minister Lester B. Pearson's 1966 *White Paper on Immigration*

Prime Minister Pearson's 1966 *White Paper on Immigration* (hereafter *"White Paper"*) was a revamping of Canada's immigration policy in order to adapt to economic shifts of industry, from a low-skill dominated market to a more industrialized and skilled worker-based economy that focused on manufacturing, management, professional, and technical occupations.[25] Essentially, technological innovation was improving at a rapid rate, while low-skill and under-employed immigration was steadily growing. What resulted was an economy that desperately needed more high-skill workers, but had far too many unskilled workers, which led to an unutilized labour marked and a high unemployment rate.[26]

migration-regulations-order-in-council-pc-1962-86-1962>. [1962 Museum].
20. *Immigration Regulations*, Order-in-Council PC 1962-86, 1962 [1962 Regulations],
21. *Supra* at Museum of Immigration,
22. "Forging our Legacy: Canadian Citizenship and Immigration, 1900-1977", online" Citizenship and Immigration Canada < http://www.cic.gc.ca/english/resources/publications/legacy/chap-6.asp?_ga=1.163997631.1446041918.1431629880#chap6-1 >. [CIC Legacy],
23. *Supra* 1962 Regulations,
24. *Ibid,*
25. *Supra* CIC Legacy,
26. *Ibid.*

The *White Paper* was created as part of the solution to this dilemma. It focused on manipulating immigration flows by preventing an explosive growth in the unskilled labor force, and by tightening sponsorship programs to prevent unskilled family members of recent immigrants from entering.[27] However, the restrictions on sponsorship had ethnic ties, as select countries were exempt from them.

In terms of the development of a policy of criminal inadmissibility, the *White Paper* also called for the removal of barriers for those who were not dangerous, such as homosexuals and chronic alcoholics, while enhancing barriers against criminals.[28] Furthermore, the *White Paper on Immigration* called for less discretionary power and the creation of an impartial system that prohibited classes could navigate. These suggestions have had lasting effects on the evolution of criminal inadmissibility, as they have helped to shape the current system.[29]

In 1967, the point system was introduced so that potential immigrants could know whether or not they had enough points to enter Canada. The categories included: education and training, personal character, occupational demand, occupational skill, age, pre-arranged employment, knowledge of French and English, the presence of a relative in Canada, and employment opportunities in the area of destination.[30] On top of the point system came the 1967 amendment to include a review board for all applicants, regardless of which prohibited class they were in. These amendments drastically increased immigration by partially removing the uncertainty that accompanies indiscriminate decision-making.[31]

G. The Immigration Act, 1976

The Immigration Act, 1976 set the tone for Canada's current immigration policy. The two major changes that this Act brought were: (1) planned immigration and (2) clear principles and objectives. First, planned immigration came in the form of projected numbers of immigrants to be allowed in for each of the four basic categories: humanitarian class, family class, independent class, and assisted relatives.[32] This is important because it demonstrates the government's willingness to let in a certain number of people. This change, tied with the ability for immigrants to apply prior to arrival, made people feel less anxious about the process of moving to a new country. Second, the Act spelled out the fundamental principles of the country's immigration policy, which included the promotion of

---

27. *Ibid.*
28. "White Paper on Immigration, 1966", online: Canadian Museum of Immigration at Pier 21 < http://www.pier21.ca/research/immigration-history/white-paper-on-immigration-1966>. [1966 Museum].
29. *Ibid.*
30. *Supra* CIC Legacy.
31. *Ibid.*
32. *Ibid.*

"Canada's demographic, economic, cultural, and social goals," including family reunification, international obligations to refugees, and non-discrimination.[33]

H. *Immigrant and Refugee Protection Act*, 2002–Present

The *Immigration and Refugee Protection Act* (hereafter *IRPA*) was enacted with the explicit purpose of striking a balance between welcoming newcomers and strengthening national security and public safety.[34] However, many legal scholars, community activists, and political commentators have criticized the Act for prioritizing national security at the expense of tolerance. This imbalance can be seen in the tools that the Act introduced or reintroduced, such as increased border security in the form of front-end security screening for all refugee claimants, broader grounds for detention, greater Ministerial discretion, fewer appeals and opportunities for the courts to delay the removal of serious criminals, and suspension of refugee claims for people charged with serious crimes."[35]

Sections 33 to 43 of the *IRPA* determine inadmissibility, while Section 36 dictates criminal inadmissibility.[36] The provisions and regulations explained in this book are based on the *IRPA*, since it is the most current immigration act. The specific focus of the book will be on criminal inadmissibility, with a particular focus on the effect of inadmissibility on American citizens. We will be examining relevant actors, practical realities, legal strategies, and case examples thoroughly throughout the rest of the book.

1.2 Important Actors

Immigration, Refugees and Citizenship Canada (IRCC—formerly known as Citizenship & Immigration Canada, CIC) oversees the application of immigration legislation in Canada. IRCC facilitates the arrival of immigrants by providing concise information and call centers for questions, but it also offers services and programs for newcomers and protects refugees. Furthermore, the IRCC grants citizenship, issues travel documents, and promotes multiculturalism.

Canada Border Services Agency (CBSA) is a federal agency that is responsible for border enforcement, immigration enforcement, and customs services. Within Canada, CBSA officers control admission at ports of entry (POEs) and screen for inadmissibility. Overseas, CBSA officers focus primarily on assessing applications sent to consulates and visa offices.[37] The CBSA also manages back-

---

33. *Ibid.*
34. Mario D. Bellisimo, *Canadian Citizenship and Immigration Inadmissibility: Criminal Law Edition* (Toronto: Thomson Reuters) at 1-3 [Mario].
35. *Ibid* at 1-3.
36. *The Immigration and Refugee Protection Act of Canada*, Canada 2014, s 33–43 [IRPA].
37. *Supra* Mari at 1-5 to 1-6.

ground checks and other immigration investigations for refugee and immigrant applicants, admissibility hearings, pre-removal risk assessments, removals, and removal order appeals.[38]

1.3 Standards of Proof in Criminal Inadmissibility Cases

The Canadian legal system employs three standards of proof in civil and criminal cases. The standard of proof will vary depending on the applicant's situation.

Beyond a Reasonable Doubt is the *criminal standard* of proof. This is the strictest possible standard of proof. Beyond a Reasonable Doubt is not a standard used in Canadian immigration law.

Balance of Probabilities is the *civil standard of proof for questions of law.* It is the standard used for most administrative tribunals. It means that the evidence presented must show that the facts as alleged are **more probable than not**. Accordingly, a party having the burden of proof by a "balance of probabilities" must be able to persuade that the evidence presented outweighs opposing evidence.

Balance of Probabilities is a higher standard of proof than Reasonable Grounds to Believe, but is lower than the criminal standard of Beyond a Reasonable Doubt."[39] Questions of law are decided on the balance of probabilities and are reviewed on the correctness standard.

Reasonable Grounds to Believe is the standard of proof for *questions of fact*, i.e. the findings of fact made by a tribunal.[40] Unless otherwise provided, inadmissibility may be based on facts for which there are reasonable grounds to believe that they have occurred, are occurring, or may occur.

The Supreme Court of Canada (SCC) has stated that the Reasonable Grounds to Believe standard requires "something more than mere suspicion, but less than the standard applicable in civil matters of proof on the balance of probabilities."[41] In essence, reasonable grounds will exist where there is an objective basis for the belief which is based on compelling and credible information.[42]

In the case of a foreign national, an officer must be satisfied that there are reasonable grounds to believe that an act has occurred. Permanent residents will be assessed by the higher Balance of Probabilities standard.

---

38. *Ibid* at 1-6.
39. http://www.cic.gc.ca/english/resources/manuals/enf/enf02-eng.pdf
40. *Moreno v. Canada* (Minister of Employment and Immigration), [1994] 1 F.C. 298 (C.A.), at para 311.
41. *Mugesera v. Canada* (Minister of Citizenship and Immigration), [2005] 2 S.C.R. 100, at para 114.
42. *Ibid.*

1.4 The Effects of 9/11 on Criminal Inadmissibility and Canadian Immigration

After the events that unfolded on September 11th, 2001, Canada was widely criticised for having an overly porous border that could easily perpetuate further terrorist activity and act as a haven for terrorism. In response to these critiques, Canada enacted Section 3(1) (*i*), which lists one of the objectives of the *IRPA* as: "to promote international justice and security by fostering respect for human rights and by denying access to Canadian territory to persons who are criminals or security risks."

The government enacted several changes within the IRPA to deal specifically with security threats, including streamlining the security certificate process to expedite removals, creating one process for all security threats, making the upholding of a certificate by the federal court an automatic removal order, executing suspension of immigration proceedings in security certificate cases and suspension or termination of a claim for protection, broader provisions on organized crime, elimination of appeals, and streamlining the removal process.[43] Furthermore, the Canadian government responded with Bill C-36, *The Anti-Terrorism Act*, which together with the *IRPA* created Canada's two-prong contribution to the "War Against Terror".[44]

Despite this two-pronged assault against terrorism and the increased border security between the United States and Canada, there were minimal immediate effects on immigration. In 2002, a year after 9/11, Professor Howard Adelman argued, "9/11 had virtually no impact on Canadian immigration policies. The overall total for immigrants remained the same, though there was a small shift within the categories to increase the numbers of skilled workers as well as parents and grandparents within the family class."[45] However, the IRPA has since defined 'terrorists' as coinciding with the Canadian *Criminal Code* definition in Section 121.1(1), and their inadmissibility is defined in Section 14 of the *Immigration and Refugee Protection Regulations*.[46] Thus, while total immigration numbers have not been largely impacted by 9/11, social perceptions of immigrants have changed, as has the screening process, leading to harsher regulations and more rigorous security checks.

---

43. *Ibid* at 1-13.
44. *Supra* Mario at 1-11.
45. Howard Adelman, "Canadian Borders and Immigration Post 9/11" (2002) 36 International Migration Review 13 at 22. [Adelman].
46. *Supra* IRPA at s 121.1(1); Henry Goslett & Barbara Caruso, *The Annotated Immigration and Refugee Protection Act of Canada* (Toronto: Thomson Reuters, 2014) at 583.

Chapter 2

Determining Criminal Inadmissibility

Under Canadian law, non-citizens **do not** have an unqualified right to enter or remain in Canada. Typically, Americans traveling to Canada do not need to obtain a visa to enter as a visitor for up to a six-month period. However, in order to work or study they will need to obtain a specific permit.

Non-Canadian citizens may be denied entry into Canada for, among other reasons, criminal convictions and criminal records. The objectives expressed in the *Immigration and Refugee Protection Act* (hereafter *IRPA*) indicate an intent to prioritize the security of Canada and Canadians. This objective is given effect by limiting the ability of foreign nationals with criminal records from entering Canada, making them inadmissible on the grounds of criminality.

For the purposes of inadmissibility, the offence on record must be an offence of a certain severity under Canadian law. How the offence is classified in a foreign jurisdiction does not matter – i.e., in order for an offence to render someone inadmissible, it (1) must be an offence under Canadian law, and (2) must be of a certain severity. For example, adultery is an offence in the Philippines but not in Canada, thus a person convicted of committing adultery in the Philippines will not be inadmissible to enter Canada based on that charge.

DUIs are one of the most common offences in the United States. Since they are the most common cause of inadmissibility to Canada, they will be the focus of this chapter, specifically, and of the book more generally.

2.1 Overview of Canadian Criminal Law

There are three classifications of criminal offences in Canada: (1) **summary offences**, (2) **indictable offences**, and (3) **hybrid offences**. Understanding how an offence is classified by Canadian law is the first step to determining whether there are likely to be any restrictions on entry into Canada.

Each provision of the *Criminal Code* details how the offence is classified and, subsequently, how it is punishable by law. In addition to the Code, there are other pieces of federal legislation that include criminal offences, such as the *Controlled Drugs and Substances Act* and the *Youth Criminal Justice Act*.

The three classifications of offences found in the *Criminal Code* are detailed below.

(1) **Summary offences** encompass the most minor offences in the *Criminal Code*. Summary offences are so minor on the scale of criminal offences that a conviction for a single summary offence would not render a person inadmissible. They are typically punishable by a fine of up to $5,000.00 and up to six months jail time. Examples of summary offences include:

- Causing a disturbance by being drunk (Section 175 (1)(a)(ii) *Criminal Code*)
- Found in a common bawdy-house (Section 210 (2)(b) *Criminal Code*)

(2) **Indictable offences** encompass the more serious offences in the *Criminal Code*. Indictable offences are subject to harsher penalties than summary offences. Offences that are prosecuted by way of indictment may be subject to a preliminary inquiry, whereby the prosecution must establish that there is sufficient evidence to bring the case to trial. The accused will also have a choice (called

"election") to be tried in a superior court by a judge and a jury, or at a provincial court by a judge presiding alone.

Examples of indictable offences include:

- Aggravated sexual assault (Section 273(1) *Criminal Code*)
- Dangerous driving, where injury or death occurs (Section 249 (3) *Criminal Code*)

(3) Most of the offences in the Criminal Code are **hybrid offences** (also known as "dual process offences"), meaning that they can be prosecuted either by summary conviction or indictment. Hybrid offences are considered indictable until the Crown (i.e. the prosecution) makes its election. The choice of whether to try the offence as indictable or summary depends largely on the facts of the case. Importantly, hybrid offences are always considered indictable for Canadian immigration purposes.

Examples of hybrid offences include:

- Impaired driving with 5ng or more of THC per ml of blood (Section 253 (3)(a) *Criminal Code*)
- Driving while disqualified (Section 259 (4) *Criminal Code*)
- Assault with a weapon or causing bodily harm (Section 267, *Criminal Code*)

2.2 Grounds for Inadmissibility

Section 36 of the *Immigration and Refugee Protection Act* (*IRPA*) outlines the grounds for criminal inadmissibility. Having committed any of the offences described by s. 36, the applicant is inadmissible to enter Canada. Additionally, one (1) hybrid offence will render a person inadmissible. On the other hand, one (1) summary conviction does not make someone inadmissible.

The first part of this section details the grounds for inadmissibility under Section 36 of the *IRPA*. The second part briefly outlines the possibility of removing the inadmissibility restriction through rehabilitation or record suspension.

A. Defining Inadmissibility under Section 36 *IRPA*

Section 36 of the *IRPA* outlines the grounds for criminal inadmissibility. The regulation is split into two sections: (1) serious criminality and (2) criminality. Restrictions on entry vary depending on how the offence is classified; therefore, classification is one of the determining factors in inadmissibility.

1. Serious criminality

"Serious Criminality" is defined in Section 36(1) as follows:

A permanent resident or a foreign national is inadmissible on grounds of serious criminality for:

(a) Having been convicted in Canada of an offence under an Act of Parliament punishable by a maximum term of imprisonment of at least 10 years, or of an offence under an Act of Parliament for which a term of imprisonment of more than six months has been imposed;

(b) Having been convicted of an offence outside Canada that, if committed in Canada, would constitute an offence under an Act of Parliament punishable by a maximum term of imprisonment of at least 10 years; or

(c) Committing an act outside Canada that is an offence in the place where it was committed and that, if committed in Canada, would constitute an offence under an Act of Parliament punishable by a maximum term of imprisonment of at least 10 years.

In order to understand whether an offence committed abroad is classified as "serious criminality" in Canada, one needs only look to the particular sentencing scheme under Canadian law; only the Canadian sentencing is relevant.

Unpacking the Provision

There are differences between offences committed inside and outside of Canada. Please see table below for further explanation.

36(1)(a)	Applies to convictions *in* Canada:
	I) Persons sentenced to more than six months in prison.
	II) Persons who have been convicted of an offence for which there is a maximum term of at least 10 years imprisonment, regardless of whether they were sentenced to serve the entire possible term.
	For example: Assault causing bodily harm
36(1)(b)	Applies to convictions *outside* of Canada:
	I) Persons convicted of an offence that, if committed in Canada, would be punishable by a maximum term of imprisonment of at least 10 years.
	For example: Fraud over $5,000.00; DUI

36(1)(c)	Applies to offences committed *outside* of Canada: I) Persons who commit an offence, **regardless of whether or not they were convicted**, that if committed in Canada would be punishable by a maximum term of imprisonment of at least 10 years.

2. Criminality

"Criminality" is defined in Section 36(2) as follows:

A foreign national is inadmissible on grounds of criminality for:

(a) Having been convicted in Canada of an offence under an Act of Parliament punishable by way of indictment, or of two offences under any Act of Parliament not arising out of a single occurrence;

(b) Having been convicted outside Canada of an offence that, if committed in Canada, would constitute an indictable offence under an Act of Parliament, or of two offences not arising out of a single occurrence that, if committed in Canada, would constitute offences under an Act of Parliament;

(c) Committing an act outside Canada that is an offence in the place where it was committed and that, if committed in Canada, would constitute an indictable offence under an Act of Parliament; or

(d) Committing, on entering Canada, an offence under an Act of Parliament prescribed by regulations.

Unpacking the Provision

There are differences between offences committed inside and outside of Canada. Please see table below for further explanation.

36(2)(a)	Applies to offences committed *in* Canada: I) Persons convicted of an offence punishable by indictment. *For example:* Theft over $5,000.00. II) Persons convicted of two offences not arising out of a single occurrence. *For example:* Theft & Assault causing bodily harm

36(2)(b)	Applies to offences committed *outside of* Canada:
	I) Persons convicted of an offence that would be classified as "indictable" in Canada.
	     For example: Theft over $5,000.00
	II) Persons convicted of two offences not arising out of a single occurrence.
	     For example: Theft & Criminal Mischief over $5,000.00

36(2)(c)	Applies to offences committed *outside of* Canada: I) Persons who have committed an act **regardless of if they were convicted**, that if committed outside of Canada would be punishable by indictment.
36(2)(d)	Applies to offences committed *while entering* Canada" I) Persons who commit a criminal offence while coming into Canada—**a conviction is not required.** *For example:* Misrepresenting that you do not have a criminal conviction on your record, when in fact you do.

B. "Committing an Act" Provisions

As previously discussed, individuals may be found inadmissible as a result of criminal convictions **or** as a result of committing an offence *where there was not necessarily a conviction.* The provisions regulating the latter type of situations are known as "committing an act" provisions.

The practical application of the "committing an act" provisions is to deny entry into Canada to persons against whom there is evidence of criminal activity that could result in a conviction if there were a prosecution in Canada.[1] For instance, this would apply in circumstances where stoning someone to death is excused in the foreign country because of adultery, but would be considered murder if it occurred in Canada. It is important to note that these provisions apply only to offences that are considered to be indictable offences (i.e. punishable by a maximum term or imprisonment of at least 10 years).

The "committing an act" provision is also applicable for pending charges or convictions, i.e. where there is a warrant out for the person's arrest, the trial is pending or ongoing, or where foreign authorities have indicated that charges may be laid. As such, a person may be inadmissible without a conviction.

The "committing an act" inadmissibility provisions would generally be applied in the following scenarios:

---

1.   http://www.cic.gc.ca/english/resources/manuals/enf/enf02-eng.pdf (3.5) page 9.

- An officer is in possession of intelligence or other credible information indicating that the person committed an offence outside Canada;
- Authorities in the foreign jurisdiction indicate that the alleged offence is one where charges would be, or may be, laid;
- The person is the subject of a warrant where a formal charge is to be laid;
- Charges are pending;
- The person has been charged but the trial has not concluded;
- The person is fleeing prosecution in a foreign jurisdiction;
- A conviction has been registered for the offence; however, a certificate of conviction is not available.

The "committing an act" inadmissibility provision would generally not be applied in the following scenarios:

- In most cases, when authorities in the foreign jurisdiction indicate they would not lay a charge or make known to an officer their decision or intent to drop the charges;
- The trial is concluded and no conviction results (for example, acquittal, discharge, deferral);
- The person admits to committing the act but has received a record suspension or the record is expunged;
- The act was committed in Canada.

The "committing an act" provisions are not to be used where a conviction has been registered and where the appropriate evidence of conviction has been obtained. Additionally, these provisions cannot be used where the person has been acquitted, or where a court has made a finding of not guilty.

C. Federal Criminal Offences v. Provincial Regulatory Offences

Canada has a division of powers between federal and provincial jurisdictions. Criminal law is under the exclusive jurisdiction of the federal government and is set out under the *Criminal Code* of Canada. There is one *Criminal Code* for all of Canada, regardless of which province or territory the offence was committed in. Additionally, as previously stated, there are several other pieces of federal legislation that include criminal offence provisions, such as the *Income Tax Act*. Committing an offence that is prescribed under these acts may also lead to inadmissibility.

The provinces may enact their own regulatory offences through provincial legislative acts and municipal by-laws. However, these offences are not considered criminal acts and do not go on your criminal record. Provincial offences tend to be minor and regulatory, while criminal offences are more severe.

The Provincial Offenses Act (POA) has three parts: the first and second parts relate to minor offences and parking infractions that are commenced by a certificate of offence. These include parking tickets or parking violations settled with fines, for which the violator can either pay the fine or have a hearing. The third part of the Act sets out the procedures for offences that are serious enough that the accused must attend court to answer to the charge.

D. Youth Offenders

In Canada, a young offender is classified as someone who is between the ages of 12 and 18. Juvenile convictions typically do not lead to criminal inadmissibility; however, under certain circumstances youth offenders may be inadmissible as a result of criminality.

Youth offenders are *admissible to Canada* as long as they were:

- Convicted in Canada under the *Young Offenders Act* [repealed] or the *Youth Criminal Justice Act* [current], *unless they received an adult sentence*,
- Treated as a young offender in a country which has special provisions for young offenders, or
- Convicted in a country which does not have special provisions for young offenders, but the circumstances of the conviction are such that they would not have received an adult sentence in Canada.

Youth offenders are **inadmissible to Canada** if they were:

- Convicted in adult court in a country that has special provisions for young offenders, or
- Convicted in a country which does not have special provisions for young offenders but the circumstances of your conviction are such that you would have been treated as an adult in Canada.

When in doubt about whether an offence committed by a minor will result in inadmissibility, check whether it appears on an FBI or fingerprint-based background check. DUIs are usually treated as adult offences, since alcohol and driving are both "adult" activities.

2.3 Interplay Between Criminal Law and Immigration Law

A. Serious v. Non-Serious Criminality

1. Non-serious criminalities

Any offence under a Federal Statute that is punishable by a maximum jail sentence of less than 10 years is a non-serious criminality.

If fewer than 10 years have elapsed from the completion of the sentence and/ or there is more than one conviction on the record, a Criminal Rehabilitation application will be required for immigration, visitation, or work permit purposes.

Examples of non-serious criminalities: theft under $5000.00, simple assault, and fraud under $5000.00.

2. Serious criminalities

Serious criminality is typified when an offense results in a maximum punishment of at least 10 years imprisonment (or equivalent offense abroad), or when an individual is criminally convicted in Canada and a term of imprisonment of more than six months has been imposed. If an individual is convicted of a serious criminality, they can never be deemed rehabilitated through the passage of time, instead they must **always apply for Criminal Rehabilitation.**

Examples of serious criminalities: offences that involve bodily injury, damage, or use of a weapon. Additionally, under Section 320.19 of the *Criminal Code* which takes effect in December 2018, a DUI offence, and/or non-compliance with a police demand concerning dangerous driving (e.g. refusing a breathalyzer test), is now also considered under the classification of serious criminality.

B. Defining Canadian Equivalence

Foreign convictions and laws are equated to Canadian law for the purposes for determining inadmissibility. Thus, in order to determine if your offence makes you inadmissible, you must first find its Canadian equivalent. Once you determine the equivalent, you can then determine how an offence will be classified (discussed below).

One cannot assume the equivalence to a foreign offence of which the essential elements are not known.

"Equivalencing" is the exercise of finding a Canadian offence that is the equivalent of the foreign offence underlying a conviction outside of Canada. In order for a foreign conviction to render a person criminally inadmissible, the activity must be a crime in both the place where it was committed and in Canada.

Determining the Canadian equivalency is crucial because an offence committed abroad that may be treated as serious in a foreign country may be classified less seriously in Canada, or may not be considered an inadmissible offence.

Individuals with a criminal history should verify their entry status regardless of offence, because even seemingly minor offences can cause inadmissibility. Unlike in the United States, Canadian criminal law does not distinguish between misdemeanor and felony offences; as such, even a misdemeanor can result in inadmissibility.

1. Steps for determining equivalency

There is no one standard formula for determining equivalency between Canadian and foreign law.[2] One must determine whether the offence, act, or omission would, if committed in Canada, constitute an offence that is punishable under *federal statute* in Canada.[3] Indeed, the determination often requires several considerations, including:

- **Text analysis**—comparing the wording of the two statutes (i.e. the Canadian *Criminal Code* and the foreign legislation) with a view to determining the "essential elements" of the respective offences.
- **Examining the facts of the case**—considering the circumstances and context surrounding the offence in relation to the *Criminal Code* provisions.

The following Federal Court jurisprudence outlines specific principles to be followed when determining equivalency for foreign convictions:

Brannson v. Canada (Minister of Employment and Immigration) [1981][4]:
- One must expect differences in the wording of statutory offences in different countries.
- One must determine the **essential elements of each offence** and be satisfied that they correspond, regardless of whether the names of the offences coincide.
- **Where the foreign offence is "broader" than the Canadian offence**, it may be possible to make a finding of equivalency if, based on the evidence, the facts establish that the actual activity for which the person was convicted falls within the scope of the Canadian offence.
- The validity or merits of the conviction should not be considered.

---

2.   However, a step-by-step break-down can be found in the detail on page 22.
3.   http://www.irb-cisr.gc.ca/Eng/BoaCom/references/LegJur/Documents/RoaAmr08_e.pdf (page 4).
4.   *Brannson v. Canada (Minister o Employment and Immigration)*, [1981] 2 F.C. 141 (C.A.), at 152–154, 145.

Hill v. Canada (Minister of Employment and Immigration) [1987][5]:

Equivalency can be determined three ways:

- By comparison of the precise wording of the essential ingredients in each statute both through documents and, if available, through the evidence of an expert in the foreign law.
- By examining the evidence adduced before the adjudicator, both oral and documentary, to ascertain if it was sufficient to establish the essential ingredients of the offence in Canada.
- By a combination of one and two.

Li v. Canada (Minister of Citizenship and Immigration) [1997][6]:

Mr. Li had been convicted of offences under the Hong Kong *Prevention of Bribery Ordinance* and sentenced to four years imprisonment. He then sought entry into Canada. In order to determine equivalency, the Adjudicator compared the essential elements of the offences and found that "corruptly" was akin to "without lawful authority or reasonable excuse". He was subsequently found to be inadmissible.

On appeal, the issues before the court were:

(1) Whether the test of equivalence of an offence under foreign and Canadian law requires a comparison of both the elements of, and defences to, each offence, under the respective laws of each country; and (2) whether there must be an equivalence of burdens of proof, in respect of the trial of the offences being compared, in order for those offences to be equivalent.

Tran v. Canada (Public Safety and Emergency Preparedness)[2017][SSC 50][7]:

In the assessment of whether an offence should be classified as **serious criminality**, consideration will be made regarding the law in place at the time of the offence; however, only convictions which took place **in Canada** are deliberated in this manner. For example, with the amendments made to the *Criminal Code* due to the passing of Bill C-46 (June 21, 2018), an offence of impaired driving which took place in Canada and before the new penalties were enforced (December 18, 2018), will continue to be treated as criminality rather than serious criminality.

The Court of Appeal held:

5.   *Hill v. Canada (Minister of Employment and Immigration) (1987)*, 1 Imm. L.R. (2d) 1 (F.C.A.), at 9.
6.   *Li v. Canada (Minister of Citizenship and Immigration)* [1997] 1 F.C. 235 (C.A.), at 249, 256–258.
7.   *Tran v. Canada* (Public Safety and Emergency Preparedness)[2017][SSC 50]

- The fundamental question in determining equivalency is: **would the acts committed abroad and punished there have been punishable here?**
- A comparison of the "essential elements" of the respective offences requires a **comparison of the definitions of those offences** *including defences* particular to those offences.
- What must be compared are the factual and legal criteria for establishing the offence both abroad and in Canada. Procedure and evidentiary rules should not be compared.

  There is no obligation to consider the constitutionality of foreign criminal law.
- If there is no equivalency of defences, and the defences available in Canada are "broader" than those available in a foreign jurisdiction, this could result in a finding that there is no equivalency.

Steps in Analysis[8]

For foreign convictions, where the foreign law is available:

1. Has the person been convicted of an offence outside Canada?
2. What are the essential elements or ingredients of the foreign offence?
3. What are the essential elements or ingredients of the suggested Canadian equivalent offence?
4. Are these same elements present in the Canadian offence as in the foreign offence?
   - If the essential elements or ingredients correspond in all relevant respects to those of the Canadian offence, there is equivalency—subject to possible defences (see below).
5. If the elements of the foreign and Canadian offences do not correspond:

   (a) Is the Canadian offence broader than the foreign offence?
   - If the elements of the foreign offence are contained within the scope of the Canadian offence, there is equivalency – subject to possible defences (see below).

   (b) Is the Canadian offence narrower than the foreign offence?
   - For equivalency, there must be evidence of the particulars of the foreign offence such that the conduct for which the person

---

8.   Detail taken from: http://www.irb-cisr.gc.ca/Eng/BoaCom/references/LegJur/Documents/RoaAmr08_e.pdf

was convicted falls within the scope of the Canadian offence.

6. Are there any defences available in relation to either the foreign or Canadian offence?

- If the elements, including defences, of the foreign offence correspond to those of the Canadian offence, there is equivalency.
- If there are relevant defences available in the foreign jurisdiction that are not available under Canadian law, there is equivalency as the Canadian offence is broader than the foreign offence.
- If there are relevant defences under Canadian law that are not available in the foreign jurisdiction, there is no equivalency, unless there is evidence, based on the particular facts which gave rise to the foreign conviction, that the person would not have been able to raise the broader Canadian defence.

7. Have Canadian laws changed since the foreign offence took place?

- If the criteria imposed by the Canadian Parliament at the time the offence took place would have rendered a different admissibility outcome, this may be subject to possible defences. N.B. this consideration is only relevant for convictions which took place in Canada and when determining if an offence should be considered as serious criminality (*Tran v. Canada*).

C. Where Foreign Law is Unavailable

Where there is no evidence of the foreign law, evidence can be adduced as to the factual foundation for the conviction. That evidence will then be examined to determine whether the essential elements or ingredients of the Canadian offence as described in Canada had been proven in the foreign proceedings to secure a conviction or were otherwise established on the facts.[9]

D. Inadmissible Family Members

In certain circumstances, foreign nationals[10] may be found inadmissible if a family member—either accompanying or non-accompanying—is inadmissible. Under s. 42 (1) of the *IRPA*:

---

9.   http://www.irb-cisr.gc.ca/Eng/BoaCom/references/LegJur/Documents/RoaAmr08_e.pdf at 10.
10.   This section does not apply to permanent residents, nor does it apply to protected persons within the meaning of Section 95 (2).

A foreign national, other than a protected person, is inadmissible on grounds of an inadmissible family member if
(a) their accompanying family member or,
(b) their non-accompanying family member is inadmissible.[11]

For example, this means that a woman moving to Canada to work for a Canadian company may be inadmissible if her husband has a DUI conviction within the last five years.

The officer holds the burden of proof for family inadmissibility. The standard of proof for a finding inadmissibility as a result of an inadmissible family member is "balance of probabilities". This means that the evidence presented must show that the facts alleged are more probable than not, e.g. that the evidence presented outweighs the opposing evidence. This is a higher standard of proof than "reasonable grounds to believe" but is lower than the criminal standard of "beyond a reasonable doubt".

1. Obtaining evidence for A42 (a)[12]

Evidence of an accompanying family member's inadmissibility may include:

- Direct testimony of the person concerned.
  For example: signed statutory declaration from the person concerned, an officer, or any other credible witness.
- Proof that a family member is inadmissible
  For example: certified copies of IRCC documents, such as a copy of a removal order etc.
- Copies of any visa refusal letter that may have been issued
  For example: "rejection order" or "direction to return order"
- Evidence, where relevant, that the person concerned is not a Canadian citizen or permanent resident
  For example: a direct admission by the person or documented through a statutory declaration

2. Obtaining evidence for A41 (b)[13]

Evidence of a non-accompanying family member's inadmissibility may include:

---

11. IRPA 42
12. CIC Manual 2013-09-04 (page 48) (7.26)
13. CIC Manual 2013-09-04 (page 48) (7.27).

- Direct testimony of the person concerned
  For example: a statutory declaration
- Proof of inadmissibility
  For example: certified copies of documents from IRCC or an established business evidencing non-compliance.

E. Determining How the Offence will be Classified

The three classifications of criminal offences are outlined in **Section 2.1: Overview of Canadian Criminal Law** (*see page 12*).

For offences committed in Canada, determining whether a particular offence has been prosecuted by summary conviction or indictment requires a review of the actual court documents. If an individual's sentence exceeded the maximum penalty for summary conviction, then they may assume that it was treated as an indictment. Since the *Criminal Code* has been amended many times, the classification is determined based on the law at the time the charge was laid.

If an individual was convicted of a hybrid offence **in Canada**, such as assault, they will need to order their court documents to confirm whether their conviction was tried summarily or by indictment. Although criminal law is of federal jurisdiction in Canada, criminal court records are held in provincial courts. Thus, in order to obtain the court documents you will have to contact the provincial court where the trial was conducted.

However, if the conviction was **outside of Canada** and the offence would be categorized as a hybrid offence, it will automatically be treated as an indictable offence. According to Section 34(1)(a) of the *Interpretation Act*, hybrid offences are, by default categorized as indictable, i.e.: "the offence is deemed to be an indictable offence if the enactment provides that the offender may be prosecuted for the offence by indictment."[14]

2.4 Overcoming Inadmissibility

There are several means available for overcoming inadmissibility under Canadian immigration law. The following section briefly sketches out certain methods of overcoming inadmissibility. The three main options—record suspension, temporary resident permit, and criminal rehabilitation—are discussed in greater detail in **Chapter 5: Overcoming Inadmissibility**.

A. Record Suspensions (Offences Committed in Canada)

A person who is technically inadmissible to enter Canada due to a criminal offence committed *in* Canada may relieve the restriction by obtaining a pardon or

---

14. Section 34(1)(a) *Interpretation Act* (R.S.C., 1985, c. I-21)

record suspension. The process of removing the restriction for a crime committed in Canada is outlined below. For details on the corresponding process for crimes committed abroad, see **Pardons and Expungements**.

People who committed an offence in Canada may be eligible to have their record suspended. A record suspension (formerly known as a pardon) allows people who were convicted of a criminal offence, but have completed their sentence and demonstrated that they are law-abiding citizens, to have their record set aside. A record suspension is available three years after completion of the sentence.

The Parole Board of Canada is the federal agency responsible for ordering record suspensions under the *Criminal Records Act* (CRA). If you get a Canadian record suspension, your record will no longer be searchable in the Canadian Police Information Centre (CPIC) database and you will no longer be inadmissible on criminal grounds.

For further information on Record Suspensions, see *Chapter 5: Overcoming Inadmissibility*.

B. Pardons and Expungements (Offences Committed Abroad)

If you were pardoned outside of Canada (for a crime committed elsewhere), you may still be inadmissible. Foreign discharges, expungements, or pardons are not necessarily recognized in Canada. You may also remain inadmissible if your chargers were withdrawn or dismissed, or you had an absolute or conditional discharge.

For the most part, Canada and the United States do not recognize each other's pardon and expungement policies. This means that having an American offence expunged may not erase the conviction for the purposes of Canadian immigration or traveling to Canada. Border agents will still be able to see this conviction at the border; they may also be able to see the expungement—**but they will not recognize it**. Foreign pardons are recognized when the charge, arrest, or conviction is removed from the individual's National Crime Information Center (NCIC) record.

The Federal Court of Appeal considered the question of equivalency with regards to pardons in *Canada (Minister of Citizenship and Immigration) v. Saini* [2002]. Mr. Saini was a citizen of India who was convicted in Pakistan of hijacking an Indian airliner. He was originally sentenced to death, but his sentence was later commuted to life imprisonment. After serving 10 years, he was granted parole and ordered to leave Pakistan. He came to Canada, claiming refugee status; however after learning of Saini's conviction, Canada issued a deportation order against him. While in Canadian custody, he was pardoned by the President of Pakistan and applied for judicial review of the deportation order.

The Court found that there was not enough evidence to adduce that the Pakistani legal system was similar enough to Canada's for the pardon to have effect in Canada. In comparing Canadian with foreign law regarding pardons, the Court must consider the process as well as the factual basis upon which they may be granted.[15]

The Court endorsed the following statement of the law with respect to foreign discharges or pardons:

> To summarize, our jurisprudence requires that three elements must be established before a foreign discharge or pardon may be recognized: (1) the foreign legal system as a whole must be similar to that of Canada; (2) the aim, content and effect of the specific foreign law must be similar to Canadian law; and (3) there must be no valid reason not to recognize the effect of the foreign law.[16]

As previously discussed, even in situations where the elements appear to be established, IRCC may not recognize the pardon. For instance, pardons administered by the State of California[17] will not seal, erase, or expunge your conviction from your criminal record. Thus, when you cross the border this information may be visible to the border patrol agent during a routine check. Such pardons may still render you inadmissible to Canada and will not help you avoid the immigration consequences of a criminal conviction.

Although an expungement or pardon may not resolve criminal inadmissibility to Canada, they can be used in support of an application for a Temporary Resident Permit (TRP) by demonstrating that this person is not a threat to Canada. They may also be used as proof of rehabilitation in support of a Criminal Rehabilitation application.

C. Deferred Adjudication, Suspended Imposition of a Sentence etc.

For the purposes of Canadian immigration law, the following **are not** considered convictions:

- Deferred adjudication
- Suspended adjudication
    - → Since these are not considered convictions, they do not result in inadmissibility.

---

15. *Canada (Minister of Citizenship and Immigration) v. Saini*, [2002] 1 F.C. 200 (F.C.A.), headnote.
16. *Ibid* at para 24.
17. California Penal Code 1203.4. (a) (1).

For the purposes of Canadian immigration law, the following **are** considered convictions:

- Suspended imposition of a sentence
- Deferred sentence[18]
    - → Since these are still considered convictions, they would lead to inadmissibility and require criminal rehabilitation or a TRP in order to enter Canada.

1. Conditional discharge

Though not a conviction, a conditional discharge is still evidence of guilt because the accused pleads guilty to, or is found guilty of, an offence. It appears on your criminal record for three years. In Canada, conditional and absolute discharges are defined in s. 173(1) of the *Criminal Code*:

730. (1) Where an accused, other than an organization, pleads guilty to or is found guilty of an offence, other than an offence for which a minimum punishment is prescribed by law or an offence punishable by imprisonment for fourteen years or for life, the court before which the accused appears may, if it considers it to be in the best interests of the accused and not contrary to the public interest, instead of convicting the accused, by order direct that the accused be discharged absolutely or on the conditions prescribed in a probation order made under subsection 731(2).

Conditional discharge is known by different names in different U.S. states. The table below shows whether the practical equivalent of conditional discharge exists in a given state and if so, what it is called.

State	Equivalent to Conditional Discharge?	Name
Massachusetts	Yes	Continuance Without a Finding (CWOF)
Pennsylvania	Yes	Accelerated Rehabilitative Disposition (ARD)
Washington	Yes	Stipulated Order of Continuance (SOC)

18. See: *M.E.I. v. Fenner, Charles David* (I.A.B. V81-6126).

If there is an entry on an individual's criminal record, such as a charge or an arrest that resulted in a non-conviction or acquittal, this may still require explanation at the border. The individual would benefit from obtaining a Legal Opinion Letter from a Canadian lawyer. This letter serves several functions, namely it:

- Recognizes the discrepancy on the individual's record.
- Outlines why the event is not equivalent to a conviction under Canadian law.
- Explains why it should not result in the person being deemed criminally inadmissible to Canada.

An individual may also want to acquire a legal opinion letter regarding convictions that are not considered offences in Canada, for example, possession of less than 30 grams of cannabis. These letters are a useful way of ensuring that you do not experience any unwelcome surprises at the port of entry.

In Canada, conditional discharges are not available for DUIs; however, some U.S. states allow for certain offenders to obtain this relief. The following table provides a description of deferred judgment programs available in select U.S. states:

State	Description of Program
California	• Available for first-time offenders with minor drug crimes. • **Not available for DUIs.** • Allows for the dismissal of charges without a conviction after the successful completion of probation. • Eligible crimes include: violations of the California Health and Safety Code, possession of marijuana with driving.
Colorado	• **DUI-offenders are eligible**, depending on jurisdiction. • Offered to individuals with blood-alcohol levels that can be considered "borderline". • This program can be particularly valuable because in Colorado charges involving alcohol cannot be plead down to a non-alcohol related offence.
Delaware	• **First time DUI offenders** can receive deferred judgement under the "election in lieu of trial" statute. • The charges will be dismissed upon successful completion of the program.

State	Description of Program
Iowa	• **Available for first time offenders (incl. first-time DUI offenders who have not refused a breathalyser test and whose blood alcohol content is lower than 0.15.** • Charges can be dismissed after being placed on probation without a judgement being entered. • **Individuals charged with a DUI causing injury do not qualify.**
Kansas	• **Individuals charged with a DUI are eligible for deferred prosecution through a diversion program, provided that this is their first charge and no injury was caused.** • Offenders holding a commercial driver's license are ineligible. • Charges are dismissed after the completion of conditions, including fees and alcohol treatment. • **Remains permanently on their driving record, but not their criminal record.**
Maine	• **Available for individuals with Class C, D, and E offences.** • DUI offences qualify as Class D. • Deferred disposition program results in the dismissal of charges after the successful completion of probationary conditions.
Montana	• **Option is unavailable to DUI offenders.** • **Incarceration in a detention centre is a possible probationary conditions.** • After completing all conditions, individuals may withdraw their initial guilty please and have other charges against them dismissed.

State	Description of Program
Nevada	• Has a program for individuals who have been convicted of DUIs to attend treatment and have a reduced sentence, but this program does not allow the sentence to be deferred or the conviction to be set aside in most cases. • Only a third time DUI offender can have their entry of judgment deferred to enter a treatment program, and this program can only be used once. • **To qualify for this program, the offender must be diagnosed as an alcoholic by a physician or a drug and alcohol abuse counsellor.**
North Carolina	• One requirement of deferred prosecution in North Carolina is that the **prosecutor must agree to the deferred prosecution.** • In practice, prosecutors in this state will not agree to use this program for a DWI or an aiding and abetting a DWI charge
North Dakota	• Deferred imposition of a sentence **is not available for those who have been charged with a DUI.**
Oklahoma	• **Individuals charged with a DUI are eligible**, but required to participate in an alcohol and drug substance abuse evaluation program. • Upon completion of the conditions, the individual is discharged without a conviction and the guilty plea will also be expunged from the person's criminal record.
Texas	• **Individuals charged with certain offences involving alcohol**, including driving, boating, or flying while under the influence, **are ineligible for deferred adjudication.** • Deferred adjudication program places defendants on community supervision with a chance to have their charges dismissed upon completion of their term without entering an adjudication of guilt.

State	Description of Program
Vermont	• State statutes allow a deferred sentence for a DUI charge, but in practice they are considered difficult to get as a sentencing option. **Second, third, and subsequent DUI offences do not qualify for deferred sentencing.** • Unlike in Canada and other U.S. states, there is an adjudication of guilt and a conviction. • After pleading guilty, offenders in Vermont have the possibility of having their sentencing deferred and being placed on probation. When they successfully fulfill the terms and conditions of their probation, the guilty verdict is stricken and the defendant is discharged. • Some offences, such as certain sexual assault charges, are excluded from eligibility.
Virginia	• Deferred disposition is available for: possession of alcohol by a minor, assault and battery, and domestic abuse. • **DUI offences do not qualify.**
Washington	• Deferred prosecution available for individuals whose crimes are deemed dependent on drugs or alcohol, or for individuals with a mental illness. • **For offenders with DUI charge, as a condition of the program the individual must be diagnosed as alcohol dependent and must get sober.**
Wisconsin	• In Wisconsin, a first DUI is not considered a criminal offence so long as no passenger in the car at the time of the offence was under the age of 16. • **Subsequent DUI offences are not eligible for deferred prosecution.**
Wyoming	• Deferred prosecution available in lieu of conviction. • **Available to first-time offenders only.** • Individuals who hold a commercial driver's license are ineligible. • The court does not enter a judgment of guilty, places the offender on probation, and after the conditions of the probation are completed the charges can be dismissed.

D. Acquittals and Non-Convictions

An individual is admissible to Canada and should have no problems with travel under the following circumstances:

- They have an arrest record for being charged, but never convicted of a crime;
- They were acquitted of a crime;
- They participated in a pre-trial intervention program;
- They had a conditional discharge (see below).

Although these situations should not prohibit travel, they may still present a problem for entry to Canada. For example, if an individual's criminal record has not been updated to reflect their acquittal, if the person has not paid a fine, or if a guilty disposition was on their record at any point. Again, under such circumstances, an individual would benefit from obtaining a Legal Opinion Letter from a Canadian lawyer.

However, as always, please keep in mind that admissibility is at the complete discretion of the border agent; there is a reversal of the burden of proof (*Onus Probandi*) with the applicant holding the obligation to prove that there was no conviction.

E. Convictions

The equivalence of an offence committed outside of Canada to a single summary offence under Canadian law is usually not enough to be considered criminally inadmissible to Canada.

If you have only one summary conviction in Canada, but no foreign convictions, you can apply to the Parole Board of Canada (PBC) for a record suspension.

If you have a criminal conviction in Canada AND a foreign conviction, then you may make a request for Criminal Rehabilitation. Rehabilitation means that you are not likely to commit new crimes. You can apply for Criminal Rehabilitation if **at least five years have passed** since you finished your criminal sentence. In such instances, you may submit an application for rehabilitation for any conditions or offences outside of Canada if you can provide evidence that you have submitted an application for record suspension to the Parole Board of Canada (PBC) for those offences committed within Canada.

A Legal Opinion Letter is also advisable in this situation.

The following table clarifies the meaning of certain American terminology as it is understood by Canadian immigration law:

Terminology Used	Defined
Acquittal contemplating dismissal	Not a conviction; would likely have the same effect as a conditional discharge.
Deferral of sentence	This is a conviction providing the offence equates to Canadian law; similar to a suspended sentence in Canadian law.
Deferral of prosecution	Not a conviction. A deferral indicates that no trial on the merits of the charge has been held; similar to a stay.
Deferral of judgment	Not a conviction. If the conditions imposed in the deferral are fulfilled, the final judgment rendered may be a finding of "not guilty."
Deferral of conviction	Not a conviction. It is a form of disposition equivalent to a conditional discharge in Canada.
Nolo contendre	A Latin phrase meaning "I will not contest it." It is a plea that may be allowed by the court in which the accused does not deny or admit to the charges. This plea is similar to pleading guilty and a conviction results.
Nolle prosequi	A Latin phrase meaning "I will no longer prosecute." The effect is similar to a stay of prosecution in Canada and no conviction results.
Sealed record	A sealed record is, for the purposes of IRPA, a criminal record. The fact that a sealed record exists does not in and of itself constitute inadmissibility. An officer should determine the circumstances of the sealed record by questioning the person concerned. A sealed record is usually the process used in the case of young offenders; however, a sealed record may also be used because of an agreement between the prosecutor and the defendant or in security cases.

Terminology Used	Defined
	In the state of Vermont, for example, a record may be sealed if a person abides by terms and conditions imposed by the court. A sealed record will appear on a person's "rap sheet"; however, the record will not be made public without a court order. In the case of a sealed record, an officer should ask whether the record was the result of a conviction as a minor. If the person was a minor, then it would most likely equate to an offence under the Young Offenders Act—unless the case would have been eligible for transfer to an adult court.
Convicted of several counts	Multiple convictions. Counts in the U.S. are equivalent to charges in Canadian law.
Expunged	Not a conviction. Expunged means to strike out; obliterate; mark for deletion; to efface completely; deemed to have never occurred.

F. Immigration Status of the Applicant

As a reminder, Canadian citizens have an unqualified right to enter and remain in Canada. As such, the rules regarding inadmissibility do not apply to Canadian citizens. Foreign nationals who hold Canadian citizenship or who are entitled to Canadian citizenship should obtain proof of citizenship in order to overcome inadmissibility.

Canadian citizenship is conferred *jus soli*, meaning "by birth". You are considered a Canadian citizen if:

- You were born in Canada and have not renounced your Canadian citizenship;
- You were born after 1947 to a Canadian parent and neither you nor they have renounced their Canadian citizenship.

If a person, convicted of an offence, presents themselves at the Canadian border with proof of their Canadian citizenship, they cannot be denied. Examples of proof of Canadian citizenship include:

- Canadian passport;
- Canadian citizenship certificate;

- Canadian-issued birth certificate;
- Proof that you were born in Canada after February 14, 1977 and neither of your parents was a Canadian citizen or permanent resident, and at least one parent had status as a diplomat in Canada;
- Naturalization certificate, issued before January 1, 1947;
- Registration of birth abroad certificate issued between January 1, 1947 and February 14, 1977, inclusively;
- Certificate of retention, issued between January 1, 1947 and February 14, 1977, inclusively.

Therefore, obtaining proof of Canadian citizenship may be an easy way of overcoming inadmissibility.

G. Whose Call is it Anyway: Understanding Who is Making Admissibility Decisions

Canada Border Services Agency (CBSA) agents have full discretion when deciding the admissibility of a foreign individual at the border. It is important to remember that border officers are not lawyers or judges and have limited experience interpreting the law. As such, they may not be inclined to consider sophisticated legal arguments about non-equivalence of statutes or for alternative dispositions, even if strictly speaking under the law, the argument is sound.

Consulates will typically have the best-trained agents and more time to evaluate an application. International airports and large land crossings will also usually have more senior officers. The burden of proof is on the applicant to prove that they are not inadmissible. If the border agent catches an individual in a lie, the individual could become permanently inadmissible to Canada.

There are four databases that the CBSA uses at Ports of Entry: Integrated Customs Enforcement System ("ICES"), Field Operations Support System ("FOSS"), Canadian police Information Center ("CPIC"), and National Crime Information Center ("NCIC").

ICES is a CBSA databases that, amongst other things, contains information about Canadians who have come into contact with CBSA or individuals who might seek to enter the country and might pose a risk. It also includes traveler records and information on customs seizures for a period of five years. FOSS is the shared database between IRCC and CBSA; it contains all of the records of the agencies' contacts with non-Canadian citizens. Specifically, it includes any immigration records and violations including pending deportation, overstays by visitors, Interpol information of suspected and known terrorists, and warrants. CPIC is the database used by Canadian law enforcement agencies; it contains criminal records and arrest warrant details. NCIC is a somewhat comparable database used by American law enforcement agencies. Notably, on December 13, 2012, Canada signed a Treaty with the USA to forge an information sharing agreement, allowing immigration authorities to easily access information regarding any criminal history of citizens from either country. Both CPIC and NCIC contain information regarding existing and expired "wants and warrants" and additional information including details of individuals the law enforcement agencies consider to be armed and dangerous.[19]

---

19. *Martin-Ivie v. Canada (Attorney General)*, 2013 FC 772 (CanLII) at para 25 [Martin-Ivie].

Chapter 3

Practice Tips for American Criminal Defense Lawyers/ Attorneys

Synopsis
3.1 Pleading Down
    A. Driving Offences
    B. Cannabis Possession Offences
    C. Hunting and Fishing Violations
3.2 Shortening Sentences
3.3 Classes and Rehabilitation Programs

Temporary Resident Permits and Criminal Rehabilitation applications can help a client get into Canada after they have already been convicted. Before the client is convicted, there are several things that a criminal defense attorney outside of Canada can do to help their clients mitigate the effects of future admissibility to Canada while facing the original criminal charge in their respective country of origin. When faced with the possibility of criminal inadmissibility, defense attorneys should pursue one of the following three options:

1. **Pleading the charge down to a lesser offence**
   → This can help the client avoid inadmissibility by pleading down to the equivalent of a summary or provincial offence, i.e. a conviction that would not result in inadmissibility.
2. **Reducing the length of the sentence (including probation)**
   → This avenue does not remove inadmissibility, but serves to shorten the length of time that the client will be inadmissible.
3. **Demonstrating that the client has been rehabilitated**
   → This tactic neither removes nor shortens the period of inadmissibility; rather, it consists of counseling clients on steps that can be taken

39

while they are inadmissible to demonstrate to the Canadian government that after the prescribed period, they are rehabilitated. This can include proof of enrollment in a class or program specifically crafted to help individuals who have committed similar crimes. This can be used to leverage the terms or length of the sentence, or it can be used as support for future immigration applications.

To summarize, here are the suggested tactics for criminal defense attorneys who are considering the impact of a sentence on their client's future admissibility to Canada. Each of the tactics will be discussed in turn.

Desired Outcome	Suggested Tactic
To prevent inadmissibility	Plead down the charge
To shorten duration of inadmissibility	Fight for a shorter sentence or alternative sentencing option
To support future immigration application	Demonstrate client's rehabilitation

3.1 Pleading Down

As previously discussed, foreign convictions are converted into a Canadian equivalent for the purposes of determining inadmissibility. There are ways to tip that conversion in your client's favor. For example, sometimes it is possible for a defense attorney to plead a client's case down to a less serious or slightly different offence; pleading down an offence can downgrade the offence from an indictable or hybrid offence to a summary offence or a provincial violation when Canadian equivalency is determined. This can have important repercussions on the client's admissibility to Canada, as it means that the offence may no longer be of the severity that would make the client inadmissible. The process of pleading down a conviction differs depending on the type of offence.

A. Driving Offences

1. Federal v. Provincial offences

Driving offences can fall under either provincial or federal jurisdiction. As previously discussed, provincial offences are less serious than federal offences and typically do not result in inadmissibility. Since there is some overlap between federal and provincial jurisdictions with regards to driving offences, defense attorneys have some room to plead down offences to avoid inadmissibility.

For example, if your client is convicted of a drunk driving offence, such as Driving Under the Influence (DUI), Driving While Intoxicated (DWI), Driving While Ability Impaired (DWAI), Operating While Intoxicated (OWI), Operating a Motor Vehicle While Intoxicated (OMVI), they will be inadmissible to enter Canada. However, there are some situations that involve drinking and driving where the offence is considered less severe.

Pleading down a driving offence often involves some creative thinking. It is important to remember that the first thing that an officer looks at when equivalencing is the text. As such, the way in which an offence is worded can make a difference in how it is treated under Canadian law. For instance, most probationary driver's licenses prohibit the holder from driving after consuming any amount of alcohol. If an individual is found "driving with the presence of alcohol in the body" whilst under a probationary license (such as a learner's permit), they may be charged with a crime. However, in Canada, restrictions pertaining to probationary licenses are the purview of the provinces, not the federal Criminal Code. As such, a conviction of driving with the presence of alcohol in the body whilst holding a probationary license would be equated to a provincial regulation and not a criminal offence, meaning that the charge would likely not lead to inadmissibility. Where available, defense lawyers should attempt to plead the charge down to something akin to "violation of a probationary license." Making this slight distinction whilst the client's trial is underway could mean the difference between being found admissible or inadmissible to Canada in the future.

What follows is a non-exhaustive list of driving offences. Remember: when challenging inadmissibility, an individual must only prove that there is no federal equivalent to their conviction. Thus, while pleading down, a defense attorney need not ensure that there is a provincial equivalent to the offence, but only that it is not an offence covered under federal statute.

Type of Offence	Provincial or Federal Jurisdiction	Inadmissible?
Driving under the influence	Federal	Yes
Driving and causing bodily harm or death	Federal	Yes
Driving while prohibited under federal law	Federal	Yes
Dangerous/careless driving	Federal	Yes
Driving while suspended under provincial law for a federal impaired driving offence	Federal	Yes

Type of Offence	Provincial or Federal Jurisdiction	Inadmissible?
Failure to provide a breath sample	Federal	Yes
Tire regulations	Provincial	No
Parking ticket	Provincial	No
Speeding	Provincial	No
Highway misconduct	Provincial	No
Handling a cell phone while driving	Provincial	No

Please Note: In many U.S. states, first offence DUIs are commonly pled down to dangerous or reckless driving offences as long as there was no motor vehicle accident or bodily harm. While a dangerous driving charge constitutes a reduction from a DUI conviction, it still constitutes a serious criminal offence under Canadian law, meaning that **the client would still be inadmissible to Canada.**

2. Blood alcohol and blood drug concentration levels

Prior to Bill C-46 (passed on June 21, 2018), dangerous driving offences in Canada were held to a maximum penalty of five years, with a 0.08% legal limit for blood alcohol content (BAC) and no specified blood-drug concentration, instead simply stating 'any impairment' while driving. For Canadian permanent residents, an imprisonment term for a driving offence which was shorter than six months, would not affect their immigration status. Additionally, foreign nationals and temporary residents of Canada, with offence records limited to a single instance of impaired driving, could be deemed rehabilitated after ten years post completion of all sentencing; effectively resolving the issue of inadmissibility to Canada.

However, as of December 18, 2018, amendments to Section 320 of the Canadian *Criminal Code* will implement harsher punishments for driving-related offences. Most pertinent to Canadian admissibility, the maximum sentence for impaired driving offences will increase from five to ten years imprisonment, subsequently also reclassifying these offences from criminality to serious criminality. This increase in penalty applies specifically to offences of: dangerous operation of a vehicle, operation while impaired, failure or refusal to comply with demand (e.g. to refuse a breathalyzer test), failure to stop after an accident, flight from a police officer, and operation while prohibited.

Consequently, individuals convicted with one of the abovementioned offences will face an increased burden in overcoming criminal inadmissibility to

Canada. Foreign nationals with even a single DUI offence will no longer be eligible for deemed rehabilitation purely through the passage of time, needing always to apply for Criminal Rehabilitation or obtain a TRP in order to gain entry to Canada.

Importantly, however, the Canadian Government has ordered special directives regarding immigration consequences for driving offences which took place prior to the effects of Bill-46. Specifically, individuals who have already been deemed rehabilitated, convicted of a single DUI offence more than ten years ago, will maintain their rehabilitated status and will not be inadmissible. Additionally, individuals who have already received approval on a prior Criminal Rehabilitation application will no longer be inadmissible regardless of when the offence occurred. Moreover, individuals convicted of a DUI offence prior to December 18, 2018, will continue to be inadmissible to Canada, though only under 36(2) non-serious criminality; therefore, individuals may still be deemed rehabilitated ten years post completion of all sentencing and may apply for criminal rehabilitation five years post completion of all sentencing.

Notably, the Canadian Minister of Immigration announced that he would issue special directives in order to mitigate the effects of Bill C-46's change to the domestic criminal law on travellers to Canada; however, as of the publication of this book, no directives have been issued. You may check the Lawyers & Judges Errata page to see if there are any current directives issued.

Offense	Outcome
Single DUI Conviction & Sentence completed more than 10 years ago (ie: Deemed Rehabilitated prior to December 18, 2018)	Maintain rehabilitated status - **Admissible**
Individual who has received an approval on a prior Criminal Rehabilitation application	Maintain rehabilitated status - **Admissible**
DUI conviction(s) - prior to December 18, 2018:	**Inadmissible** under 36(2)/ non-serious criminality ($200 processing fee on rehabilitation)
DUI conviction post December 18, 2018	**Inadmissible** under serious criminality

Furthermore, some driving offences that were already considered serious criminality will also have their maximum penalties increased from 10 to 14 years imprisonment. These offences include: vehicle operation causing bodily harm, vehicle operation while impaired causing bodily harm, failure or refusal to comply with demand after having causing a vehicle related accident resulting in bodily harm, and failure to stop after an accident resulting in bodily harm. Individuals convicted with these forms of criminal offence remain inadmissible to Canada, as they were prior to the changes.

Moreover, alongside Canada's legalization of cannabis, which took place on October 17, 2018 (*Cannabis Act*), Bill C-46 also implements greater specification regarding driving under the impairment of drugs (Section 320.14, *Criminal Code*). Three new offences are established:

1. **2 nanograms (ng) but less than 5ng of THC (lower-level):** classed as a summary conviction criminal offence and punishable by a maximum of $1,000 in fines.
2. **5ng or more of THC (higher-level):** classed as a hybrid offence that can be prosecuted either by indictment or by summary conviction.
3. **Combined THC and Alcohol (2.5ng/ml THC plus 50mg alcohol per 100ml of blood):** classed as a hybrid offence that can be prosecuted either by indictment or by summary conviction.

The above stated amendments relate to blood-drug and combined alcohol concentrations present within hours of driving.

Both hybrid offences are punishable by a mandatory penalty of $1,000 for a first offence, with escalating penalties for repeat offenders. If charged as a summary conviction, a maximum punishment of two years less a day would be implemented (increased from 18 months). In more serious cases, offence punishments will mirror those of impaired driving and adhere to the new maximum penalty of ten years imprisonment and a serious criminality classification—rendering convicted offenders inadmissible to Canada.

3. Greater Powers and New Testing Methods for Police

Previously, police were lawfully only allowed to administer a breathalyzer when under reasonable suspicion that an individual was driving under the influence of alcohol. However, the new legislation of Bill C-46, under Section 320.27 of the *Criminal Code*, now grants the police greater power by allowing random conduction of roadside alcohol breathalyzing. Additionally, alongside the legalization of marijuana, police are now equipped with screening tools to test drivers' saliva or blood for drugs in their system; however, unlike alcohol testing, a drug test may only be conducted under reasonable suspicion of drug use. Collected bodily fluid samples which are submitted for testing may serve as judicial evidence for impaired driving, without additional proof. This new legislation permits police to assume that any drug present in the impaired driver's body (up to two hours after driving) is both the case and proof of impaired status.

While the *Criminal Code* lays out standardized legal limits for blood alcohol concentrations, it should be noted that most provinces and territories have administrative laws for drivers whose BAC levels are 0.05% and over. Drivers at these levels do not face criminal charges, but they are subject to administrative penalties, for example, license suspensions, impoundments, or remedial programs.

Additionally, in regard to alcohol whereby a foreign jurisdiction sets a lower BAC limit than the *Criminal Code*, there is room to argue that a conviction in that jurisdiction should not be considered as serious in Canada, if and only if, the individual did not show signs of intoxication.

To clarify, section 253 *Criminal Code*—"Operation while Impaired"—has two parts; part *a* details that a person can be convicted if they have lost their ability to operate the vehicle properly **regardless** of whether they are at or above the legal limits for BAC (0.08%) or BDC (2ng/ml), conversely, part *b* details that someone can be convicted if their concentration is at or above the legal limits. Thus, a person can be convicted of a DUI under s. 253 if they are **visibly under the influence of alcohol or drugs**, or are above the BAC or BDC legal limit.

This has important consequences for equivalency. For example, the legal limit in Australia is 0.05% BAC. In this scenario, an individual could argue that a conviction at this level would not equate to the Canadian criminal conviction, but rather to a provincial administrative regulation. This means that someone convicted of only one alcohol related DUI in Australia would likely be admissible to Canada, as the foreign law is broader than the Canadian law and the offence does not meet the minimum requirements that are deemed necessary to violate the federal statute. Again, under such circumstances, an individual would benefit from obtaining a Legal Opinion Letter from a Canadian lawyer, to recognise the discrepancy and outline why the event is not equivalent under Canadian law.

4. Other Provincial Regulations

Regulation/ Program	Amounts to a criminal conviction?	Details
Short-term Administrative license suspension program	No	• Implemented in every province except Quebec. • Administrative license suspension (of several days to several weeks) for all drivers found driving with a BAC of 0.05% or higher. • Either immediate roadside license suspensions or reinstatement fines. • Meant to deter drivers from driving while under the influence even if they are not intoxicated enough to violate the federal statute and be subject to criminal charges.
Graduated licensing program	No	• Certain province-specific restrictions on the number of passengers a new driver can bring along and what time of day they are restricted from driving.
0.00% BAC restriction for young or novice drivers	No	• Sometimes subsumed in the "graduated licensing program." • Ensures that novice drivers gain adequate experience before being allowed to have any amount of alcohol in their system while driving.
Ignition interlock program, Vehicle impoundment program	No	• These measures restrict driving for persons who show a repeated willingness to endanger the public and violate administrative and regulatory laws.

B. Cannabis Possession Offences

On October 17th 2018, Canada became the second country in the world to legalize and regulate the sale of cannabis—the *Cannabis Act* (Bill C-45).

Prior to Bill C-45 the Canadian *Drug and Substance Act* dictated possession of less than 30 grams of cannabis to be considered a summary offence, and possession of more than 30 grams of cannabis to be an indictable offence.

Canadian law now states that it is legal to possess less than 30 grams of cannabis, which has been purchased from an authorized distributor. Exceeding the legal 30 gram limit remains an indictable offence. Additionally, the *Cannabis Act* now dictates the possession of cannabis purchased by an unauthorized distributor, regardless of quantity, to be a hybrid offence and subject to harsher consequences than prior to Canada's cannabis legalization.

1. Immigration and Cannabis Possession INSIDE Canada

For foreign nationals convicted of possessing more than 30 grams of cannabis in Canada, they will still be deemed inadmissible.

Possession of any quantity of cannabis purchased by an unauthorized distributor will render a foreign national criminally inadmissible as it is typified as a hybrid offence—for the purposes of Canadian immigration law, a hybrid offence is deemed to be an indictable offence, even if the offence was prosecuted summarily.

For foreign nationals entering Canada for cannabis tourism they are advised to ensure purchase of cannabis from authorized government distributors and keep their receipts. Foreign nationals should also be aware that it will remain illegal to bring cannabis into the country, even for medical purposes.

2. Immigration and Cannabis Possession OUTSIDE Canada

Foreign nationals with a conviction for possession of more than 30 grams of cannabis will still be inadmissible to Canada, as the Canadian equivalent has remained an indictable offence.

However, despite the fact that possessing under 30 grams of cannabis is now not an offence in Canada, and even prior to the legalization of cannabis this type of conviction would not have been rendered an inadmissible status, now individuals who commit this form of offence outside of Canada may face inadmissibility. This is due to the Canadian Government implementing much harsher punishment for possession of **any amount of illicit cannabis**. Subsequently, an individual charged with possession of less that 30 grams of cannabis in a state where all cannabis purchase is illegal, would be inadmissible on the grounds of illicit purchase, as this is the Canadian equivalent of an indictable offence.

PRIOR to cannabis legalization in Canada

Type of Offence	Inadmissible?
Possession of under 30 grams of cannabis	Not Inadmissible if this was the applicants only offence. Equivalent of summary offence in Canada
Possession of over 30 grams of cannabis	Inadmissible. Equivalent of indictable offence in Canada.

POST cannabis legalization in Canada

Type of Offence	Inadmissible?
Possession of under 30 grams of cannabis—will depend whether it is cannabis or **illicit cannabis**	Not Inadmissible on grounds of possession, as not offence in Canada. **However, inadmissible on grounds of illicit purchase as this is an indictable offence in Canada.**
Possession of over 30 grams of cannabis	Inadmissible. Equivalent of indictable offence in Canada.

The practical advice in this situation would be to argue that foreign nationals who purchase cannabis illicitly do not have the legal option like Canadians. Moreover, if their charge was based on possession, not illegal purchase, there may be room to argue an admissible status from this direction. As continually mentioned, entry to Canada is entirely at the discretion of the border agent and their interpretation of the offence.

C. Hunting and Fishing Violations

Thousands of tourists enter Canada each year for the purposes of hunting and fishing. As with other criminal charges, certain hunting and fishing violations will make you inadmissible to Canada. The regulatory scheme governing hunting and fishing is divided between federal and provincial jurisdiction. Further, municipal bylaws can impose additional restrictions and regulations on these activities. As with other types of offences, equivalency is necessary in order to determine whether a conviction will lead to inadmissibility. If the offence would be classified as either a municipal or provincial offence under Canadian law, your client will not be inadmissible (please see *Chapter 2, Section 2.2(C) "Federal Criminal Offences v. Provincial Regulatory Offences"* for more details about the difference between criminal charges and provincial administrative charges).

The following table provides a general outline of the type of offences that are governed by federal legislation, and those that fall under provincial jurisdiction. As previously noted, a violation related to one of the duties covered by provincial law will not affect your admissibility to Canada. It is helpful to plead down to an offence that would fall within provincial jurisdiction in Canada so that it will be treated as non-criminality for equivalency purposes.

Federal	Provincial
Fisheries Act: • Management and control of fisheries • Conservation of fish species • Protection of fish habitats • Protection of public health through the prevention of pollution • Imposition of gear restrictions	Administering fishing permits and licenses Deciding daily limits and possession limits on fishing Administering sport fishing Determining how fish must be packaged and transported
Migratory Birds Convention Act: • Preservation of migratory birds • Determines which species of bird can be hunted or have their nests damages • Governs licensing and general conservation of birds • Offences are often hybrid	Deciding where the harvesting of fish may legally occur
Canada Wildlife Act: • Similar to above, but for different endangered or at-risk species	Specific regulations relating to hunting, including minimum distance that a hunter must be from a road, which direction a hunter must be shooting, what garments must be worn
Firearms Act: • Who has the right to bear arms based on a license scheme	Regulating the purchase of hunting licenses by non-residents Regulating the amount of hunting that can be done in a certain area Exporting and importing game for non-residents

It is important to stay constantly updated on new legislation, as hunting regulations are updated every one or two years based on the demography of species and changes in migratory patterns. Furthermore, the *Environment Enforcement Act* is in the development stage and, if passed, will amend several federal statutes including: the *Antarctic Environmental Protection Act*, the *Canada National Marine Conservation Areas Act*, the *Canada National Parks Act*, the *Canada Wildlife Act*, the *Canadian Environmental Protection Act*, the *International River Improvements Act*, the *Migratory Birds Convention Act*, the *Saguenay-St. Lawrence Marine Park Act*, and the *Wild Animal and Plant Protection and Regulation of International and Interprovincial Trade Act*.

3.2 Shortening Sentences

As discussed above, pleading down a conviction to the equivalent of a provincial offence will remove the possibility of being found criminally inadmissible. If there is no way to plead down the offence to a less serious conviction, the next-best options are to advocate to have the sentence shortened (discussed in this paragraph) or to ensure that your client attends rehabilitation classes (discussed in the preceding paragraph). These tactics help to minimize the impact of a conviction that renders a client inadmissible. Shortening probation periods, license suspensions, jail times, and the number of community service hours needed to complete all of the terms of their sentence will allow the client to apply for criminal rehabilitation that much sooner.

Remember: an individual must complete all of the terms of their sentence, including payment of fines, before they are eligible for criminal rehabilitation. The prescribed wait period will start only after they have completed all of the terms. Thus, one way to shorten the amount of time that a client is deemed inadmissible is to ensure that they pay their fines as soon as possible. On some occasions, in an effort to shorten the sentence, defence attorneys can exchange higher fines for more probation, or agree for their client to complete a counseling program or class instead of probation.

You have completed your sentence if you have:

√ Paid all of the fines
√ Completed probation
√ Completed any court-ordered classes or programs
√ Finished mandated community service hours
√ Completed all other court-mandated conditions

Pro Tip: It is important to counsel your clients to be diligent about keeping their receipts, court records, and other files pertaining to their sentence. While it does not technically impact the length of the sentence, they will need these files in order to apply for criminal rehabilitation or a TRP, and it can be incredibly time-consuming, and sometimes fruitless, to locate them down the line.

3.3 Classes and Rehabilitation Programs

Attorneys should counsel their clients to attend classes or programs geared at rehabilitating offenders in similar circumstances. While these classes do not shorten or remove the amount of time that a client is considered criminally inadmissible, they do improve the success rate of future immigration applications. By pursuing rehabilitation, the client is demonstrating that they take responsibility for their crime and are unlikely to reoffend. The more the individual can demonstrate that they have become a responsible and valued member of the community, the greater the likelihood that their immigration application will be approved. This applies equally to applications for temporary travel as well as permanent rehabilitation.

Rehabilitation programs are created to reduce the chances of re-offending. There are a broad range of programs and approaches, each geared toward particular offenders and/or offences. These include: correctional programs, education programs, social programs, and vocational programs.

- **Correctional programs**
  Correctional programs help offenders avoid re-offending by teaching them to cope with challenges and stress without the use of drugs and/or alcohol. One example is the Canadian *High Intensity National Substance Abuse Program*, which aims to rehabilitate offenders whose convictions are directly linked to their substance abuse.[1]
- **Educational programs**
  Educational programs aim to reduce re-offending by providing personal development through the use of academia, such as adult literacy programs.[2] One Canadian example is the *Adult Basic Education Program*, which covers the core curriculum of grades 1 to 12 and provides a high

---

1. "National Substance Abuse Programs" Canadian Government Correctional Services, online: Correctional Service Canada <http://www.csc-scc.gc.ca/correctional-process/002001-2009-eng.shtml#s5>
2. "Education Programs" Canadian Government Correctional Services, online: Correctional Service Canada <http://www.csc-scc.gc.ca/correctional-process/002001-2002-eng.shtml>

school diploma upon its completion.[3]

- **Social programs**

  Social programs help offenders that are having difficulties transitioning back into their community after serving time in jail. These come in many different forms, but generally consist of social and cultural groups working with offenders in order to promote personal and social growth.[4]

- **Vocational programs**

  Vocational programs help to transition offenders into the job market upon release by providing them with the necessary skills to find work.[5] CORCAN is an example of a key vocational rehabilitation program that "contributes to safe communities by providing offenders with employment and employability skills training while incarcerated in federal penitentiaries."[6]

The appropriate combination of programs can assist with your client's rehabilitation. For example, if somebody is a repeat DUI offender that lost their job and assaulted someone whilst intoxicated, a vocational program along with a correctional program may convince an immigration officer that the client has truly been rehabilitated. Once they have completed the programs, they will have gained the necessary skills to be considered a valuable member of society.

Classes and rehabilitation programs are not the only things that can improve your client's image in the eyes of the Canadian government; successful applicants often demonstrate that they have become involved in the community by procuring reference letters attesting to good character and volunteer work.

---

3.   "Education Programs" Canadian Government Correctional Services, online: Correctional Service Canada <http://www.csc-scc.gc.ca/correctional-process/002001-2018-eng.shtml#adult>

4.   "Social Programs" Canadian Government Correctional Services, online: Correctional Service Canada <http://www.csc-scc.gc.ca/correctional-process/002001-2003-eng.shtml>

5.   "Vocational Programs" Canadian Government Correctional Services, online: Correctional Service Canada <http://www.csc-scc.gc.ca/correctional-process/002001-2004-eng.shtml>

6.   "CORCAN" Canadian Government Correctional Services, online: Correctional Service Canada <http://www.csc-scc.gc.ca/corcan/index-eng.shtml>

Chapter 4

Consequences of Being Found Inadmissible

CBSA has the power to issue removal orders against individuals who do not have the right to enter or remain in Canada. Once an individual is found inadmissible to Canada, they will not be able to enter the country without obtaining a permit or waiver, or waiting a prescribed period of time. If they are already in the country or at a port of entry, they may be subject to an official order to leave.

Removal orders may be issued for several reasons, such as a failed refugee claim or overstaying a temporary visa. **Please note: this chapter pertains solely to removal orders for reasons of criminality.** It is important to note that removal orders for reasons of criminality pertain only to offences committed outside of Canada.

4.1 Possible Outcomes at the Port of Entry if Found Inadmissible

There are four (4) possible outcomes to being found inadmissible at a port of entry. The first possibility—a **Direction to Leave Canada** order—is the least

53

serious. This order will deny the individual entry, but will not have any ancillary consequences. More serious offences will be subject to **Removal Orders**. There are three (3) types of removal orders: **Departure Orders, Deportation Orders,** and **Exclusion Orders.**

A. Direction to Leave Canada

In most cases, someone who is refused entry into Canada at a port of entry will be given a **"Direction to Leave Canada"** (commonly referred to as 'voluntary departure') and asked to leave without any further consequences. A direction to leave Canada order differs from a removal order in that it does not bar the person from reapplying for entry at any time.

However, should they attempt to re-enter the country soon after being denied, they will be expected to provide a reasonable explanation for trying again. For inadmissibility for reasons of criminality this would mean either applying for relief with a TRP or having their admissibility removed through criminal rehabilitation. In cases where the applicant maintains they are not inadmissible, they may return with proof of such.

Direction to Leave Canada orders (as they pertain to criminal inadmissibility) are typically issued for:

- Non-serious criminality issues.
- Circumstances where the person is genuinely unaware of their inadmissibility and have made an honest mistake in trying to enter Canada.
- Serious criminality, though this is unlikely unless there is a very compelling reason to permit entry.

B. Removal Orders

There are three (3) types of removal orders, namely, departure orders, exclusion orders, and deportation orders.[1]

If an individual has a serious conviction on their record, if they cause a disruption with a border immigration officer, or if they attempt repeated entry without the proper documentation, they may be subject to one of the following removal orders:

1. Departure Order

This is the first type of removal order, detailed in s. 224 *IRPR*. It requires the person to 1) **leave Canada within 30 days** after the order becomes enforceable and 2) **to confirm the departure with the CBSA.**

---

1.   Section 223 *IRPR*.

Section 224 of the IRPR is reproduced below.

224. **(1)** An enforced departure order is prescribed as a circumstance that relieves a foreign national from having to obtain authorization under subsection 52(1) of the Act in order to return to Canada.

(2) A foreign national who is issued a departure order must meet the requirements set out in paragraphs 240(1)(a) to (c) within 30 days after the order becomes enforceable, failing which the departure order becomes a deportation order.

(3) If the foreign national is detained within the 30-day period or the removal order against them is stayed, the 30-day period is suspended until the foreign national's release or the removal order becomes enforceable.

If an individual complies with the requirements of their departure order, they may reapply to enter into Canada at any time and will be subject to normal examination. To reiterate: no additional application will be required, but they will need to address the reason that they were required to leave Canada. For instance, resolving inadmissibility through rehabilitation or by obtaining the necessary permits and visas.

In *Rodrigues v. Canada (Minister of Citizenship and Immigration)*, the Federal Court considered the case of Ms. Rodrigues, a citizen of Guyana who was denied refugee status and subsequently issued a departure order. The Court took the opportunity to clarify the content of a departure order, stating:

> A person…is given an opportunity, under the legislation, to voluntarily leave the country pursuant to a departure order, before the order becomes a deportation order. If the person leaves, voluntarily, advantages arise, e.g. the ability to return without the need for a Minister's permit. This is effected by giving the individual a departure certificate when they leave.[2]

However, if they failed to complete one or both of the above requirements within the allotted time, **the departure order will automatically become a deportation order**.

Calculating 30-day period
The calculation is suspended when:

---

2.   *Rodrigues v. Canada (Minister of Citizenship and Immigration)*, 184 FTR 13, at para 5 [Rodrigues].

1) The person is detained;
   → Once an individual is released from detention, the 30-day period resumes (and any days that elapsed pre-detention are then subtracted from the remaining days).

-OR-

2) The removal order against them is stayed by a judge at the Federal Court.
   → The 30-day period resumes the day after a cancellation of the stay. The number of days within the applicable period before the stay was imposed is counted against the remaining time.

Failure to Comply with a Departure Order

If a person fails to depart by the applicable date, the departure order will automatically become a deportation order, meaning:

- The individual may be arrested for removal.
- The individual may be detained.
- The individual may be removed from Canada.

2. Deportation Order

Deportation orders are typically reserved for the most serious crimes or multiple criminal offences. A person may also receive a deportation order if their refugee claim has failed or, as previously noted, for failing to meet the requirements of a departure order. A deportation order will result in a person being **permanently barred from returning to Canada**. A deportation order obliges the foreign national to obtain a written authorization in order to return to Canada *at any time* after the deportation order was enforced.

When someone receives a deportation order, the person in question must leave Canada by a specified date and cannot return. **In order to return**, one must acquire written permission from a Canadian officer through an **Authorization to Return to Canada (ARC)** (see below). The ARC is not likely to be granted without criminal rehabilitation or a TRP.

Deportation orders are detailed in s. 226 of the *IRPA*:

226. (1) For the purposes of subsection 52(1) of the Act, and subject to subsection (2), a deportation order obliges the foreign national to obtain a written authorization in order to return to Canada at any time after the deportation order was enforced.

(2) For the purposes of subsection 52(1) of the Act, the making of a deportation order against a foreign national on the basis of inadmissibility under paragraph 42(b) of the Act is prescribed as a circumstance that relieves the foreign national from having to obtain an authorization in order to return to Canada.

3. Exclusion Order

An exclusion order typically bars the recipient from returning to Canada for one (1) year. However, individuals who are issued exclusion orders for misrepresentation cannot return for two (2) years (see *Chapter 6: Misrepresentation* for more information on what constitutes misrepresentation).

Upon completion of the prescribed wait period, the individual may enter Canada again, subject to normal examination, provided that they present a Certificate of Departure indicating the date that they previously departed Canada. If the prescribed wait period has passed, they will not need to obtain an ARC before re-entering Canada (in addition to obtaining a TRP or criminal rehabilitation if their criminality requires it).

If the recipient of an exclusion order needs to return to Canada *before* the prescribed wait period is over, they will need to obtain an ARC (see below).

4.2 Getting Through the Border after Denial of Entry for Non-Criminal Reasons

An Authorization to Return to Canada (ARC) provides individuals who are currently under a removal order from Canada with special permission to enter the country. An ARC comes in the form of a written authorization by an officer. Per s. 52 (1) *IRPA*, "if a removal order has been enforced, the foreign national shall not return to Canada, unless by an officer or in other prescribed circumstances".

Applying: An ARC application may be made in conjunction with the TRP or criminal rehabilitation application and a temporary resident visa application.

Most of the time, POEs will not process ARC applications. As such, applications should be submitted by mail to the nearest visa office.

PLEASE NOTE: An ARC only overcomes the exclusion order, not the root of the inadmissibility. As such, individuals with criminal inadmissibility must also apply for criminal rehabilitation or a Temporary Resident Permit (TRP) in order to enter Canada (see: **Chapter 5: Overcoming Inadmissibility**).

A. Who Needs to Obtain an Authorization to Return to Canada (ARC)?

Type of Order	ARC Required?	
	If the allotted time has passed and the conditions of the order have been fulfilled	If allotted time has not yet passed
Departure Order	No	No
Exclusion Order	No	Yes
Deportation Order	Yes	Yes (always need ARC)
Direction to Leave Canada	No	No (never need ARC)

B. When an Authorization to Return to Canada (ARC) is Required

1. Considerations

Neither the Act nor the Regulation specifies any criteria for the officer in charge of assessing the application for authorization to return[3], however both the case law and IRCC procedure provide some insight into the considerations.

The IRCC Operation Manual provides the following guidelines:

Section 52 of IRPA is intended to send a strong message to individuals to comply with enforceable departure orders. A permanent bar on returning to Canada is a serious consequence of non-compliance. Consequently, an Authorization to Return to Canada (ARC) should not be used as a routine way to overcome this bar, but rather in cases where an officer considers the issuance to be justifiable based on the facts of the case.

Individuals applying for an ARC must demonstrate that there are compelling reasons to consider an Authorization to Return to Canada when weighed against the circumstances that necessitated the issuance of a removal order. Applicants must also demonstrate that they pose a minimal risk to Canadians and to Canadian society. Merely meeting eligibility requirements for the issuance of a visa is not sufficient to grant an ARC.[4]

3. *Chazaro v. Canada (Citizenship and Immigration)*, [2006] FCJ No 1234 (QL), at para 19, 155 ACWS (3d) 640 (Chazaro).
4. CIC, Operation Manual, OP 1 Procedures, 18 November 2013, at para 6.1 at p 25.

Before applying for an ARC, an individual should consider whether the circumstances that led to the removal order being issued have changed. In reviewing the ARC application, an immigration officer will consider the factual circumstances of the case in relation to the objections of the Act; however, ARC applications need not be as detailed as "mini humanitarian and compassionate application[s]".[5]

If the circumstances of their removal have not changed—i.e., if they were deported because they were found working illegally in Canada and are currently unemployed in their home country—it is unlikely that the ARC will be granted. Specific Factors to Consider (non-exhaustive)[6]:

- The severity of the IRPA violation that led to the removal.
- Applicant's history of cooperation with IRCC.
- The reasons for the applicant's request to return to Canada.
- Are there factors that make the applicant's presence in Canada compelling?
- Can the applicant support themselves financially?
- How long the applicant intends to stay in Canada.

Application

If an individual is applying to come to Canada for any reason (i.e. visiting, studying, working, or migrating) the ARC will be dealt with in the same application as whatever visa they are applying for. However, the application will be subject to an additional ARC fee.

NOTE: If the Government of Canada spent money to remove the inadmissible person from the country, they will have to repay any costs before an ARC will be issued. If this is the case they will be advised once their application is in process.

4.3 When an Authorization to Return to Canada (ARC) is Not Required

A. Denied Entry for Criminal Reasons

While an ARC may not be required for certain removal orders (see above table for clarification), **an individual must resolve the criminality issues that re-**

(http://www.cic.gc.ca/english/resources/manuals/op/op01-eng.pdf)
5. *Khakh*, at para 26.
6. CIC, Operation Manual, OP 1 Procedures, 18 November 2013, at para 6.1, at p 27.

sulted in removal or denied entry before returning to Canada. This can be done through an application for Criminal Rehabilitation or a TRP (see *Chapter 5: Overcoming Inadmissibility*).

B. Effect of Pardons on Need to Apply for an ARC

Enforced removal order based solely on convictions for which a pardon has been granted.	ARC is required.
Unenforced removal order based *solely* on convictions for which a pardon has been granted.	ARC is not required.
Unenforced removal order based on convictions for which a pardon has been granted and other grounds of inadmissibility.	ARC is required.

Chapter 5

Overcoming Inadmissibility

As we have seen, certain criminal offences may make someone inadmissible to Canada. This chapter focuses on the three most comprehensive ways of overcoming criminal inadmissibility, namely: Temporary Resident Permits (TRP), Rehabilitation, and Record Suspensions.

As the name suggests, TRPs provide a temporary relief from inadmissibility, allowing the permit holder to enter Canada under certain conditions for a limited amount of time. Rehabilitation and Record Suspensions are permanent solutions to inadmissibility. However, they are only available after a certain amount of time has passed since the offence was committed and the sentence served (see below).

5.1 Entering and Remaining in Canada

As discussed in preceding chapters, non-Canadian citizens do not have an unqualified right to enter or remain in Canada. Admission of a foreign national is contingent upon several factors, one of which is criminality. It is to the discretion of the border officer whether to allow a foreign national to enter Canadian soil. The provision pertaining to right of entry is reproduced below.

Section 18 of the *IRPA* states:

18. (1) Every person seeking to enter Canada must appear for an examination to determine whether that person has a right to enter Canada or is or may become authorized to enter and remain in Canada.

(2) Subsection (1) also applies to persons who, without leaving Canada, seek to leave an area at an airport that is reserved for passengers who are in transit or who are waiting to depart Canada.

Section 20 of the *IRPA* states:

20. (1) Every foreign national, other than a foreign national referred to in section 19, who seeks to enter or remain in Canada must establish,

(*a*) to become a permanent resident, that they hold the visa or other document required under the regulations and have come to Canada in order to establish permanent residence; and

(*b*) to become a temporary resident, that they hold the visa or other document required under the regulations and will leave Canada by the end of the period authorized for their stay.

A. Visitor Visas

Depending on your nationality, you may need to apply for a visitor visa to visit Canada as a tourist. IRCC has a list of all visa-exempt countries available on their website.

Typically, **United States citizens and Green Card holders do not require a visa** to enter Canada temporarily (i.e. for a period of less than six (6) months during which they will not be working or studying).[1] This is not the case if they are found criminally inadmissible.

5.2 Temporary Resident Permit (TRP)

If you have a valid reason to travel to Canada, but you are criminally inadmissible, you may qualify for a Temporary Resident Permit (TRP). A TRP is like a "hall pass" that allows criminally inadmissible individuals to enter Canada for a specified reason and for a specified amount of time. As the name implies, TRPs are *not* a permanent solution to inadmissibility.

A Temporary Resident Permit lets you enter or stay in Canada if:

- It has been less than five years since the completion of the sentence (including jail time, community service hours, probation, and fee payment), **OR**
- More than five years have elapsed since the completion of the sentence and the individual has not applied for, nor received a negative or positive decision on an application, for criminal rehabilitation.

In summary, anyone who is otherwise inadmissible may apply for a TRP, no matter how much time has passed since the offence was committed. Once the inadmissibility has been resolved through a record suspension or criminal rehabilitation, a TRP is no longer necessary.

A. Valid Reason for Travel

An immigration or border services officer will consider whether you have a valid reason to enter Canada. They will then decide if your need to enter Canada outweighs the safety risks to Canadian society. The more Canada benefits from the visit of an inadmissible person, the more likely they are to receive a TRP. Essentially, the Canadian government is looking for a reason related to the person's work, family, or an emergency.

The definition of a "valid reason" is not outlined by IRCC; as such, it is highly discretionary on the part of the immigration officer. In fact, TRPs were formally called Minister's Permits because a minister had to sign off on it. Valid reasons for travel may include travel for work or to attend a family wedding. Leisure travel is not generally considered a "valid reason" for travel. However, many people seek to obtain TRPs in order to go on vacations with their family, such as cruises or fishing trips, and some officers are compassionate when the trip involves young children or elderly parents of an inadmissible person.

---

1. S. 190 (1)(c) *Regulations* ; section 190 (1) names the comprehensive list of foreign nationals who are exempt from requiring a visitor's visa to temporarily enter Canada.

In these situations, the success of the application often depends on where it is submitted. For instance, visa officers are often less lenient with vacation travel than border agents. Additionally, there is a high likelihood of obtaining a TRP for leisure travel when the applicant was unaware of their inadmissibility, purchased an expensive trip and applies for a TRP at the POE.

You have the highest likelihood of obtaining a TRP if:

1) Your presence in Canada will have a benefit on the Canadian economy, or

2) Your presence in Canada will benefit a Canadian citizen (i.e. attending a wedding or visiting a sick family member)

3) You work in one of the following industries:
   - Transportation industry (i.e. pilots, flight attendants, truck drivers etc.)
   - Events or sales
   - Cruise ship staff
   - Touring theatre shows, concerts, or sporting events
   - Other industries where travel is an integral part of the job, or your travel to Canada will benefit the Canadian economy

It is important not to lie about your reasons for travel in order to increase your chances of obtaining a TRP. The reasons should be well documented and proof should be provided to the information officer.

In order to obtain a TRP, the individual must disclose their true reason for entering Canada. Additionally, they must not stay longer than the time allotted for by the TRP. **Once the TRP expires, the individual is once again considered criminally inadmissible to Canada.**

B. Considerations

In addition to ensuring that the requisite time has elapsed since the sentence was served, officers will consider several other factors when deciding whether to issue a TRP, including:

- The seriousness of the offence;
- The likeliness of committing further offences;
- Evidence of reform and rehabilitation;
- Whether there is a pattern of criminal behavior (i.e. if the offence was a single event and out of character);
- If there are any outstanding criminal charges or unpaid fines;

- Eligibility for rehabilitation or record suspension (see proceeding sections);
- Risk to Canada or to Canadians;
- The number of convictions on their record;
- The severity of the offence;
- Whether the crime involved drugs (exceptions are made for marijuana or hashish possession);
- Whether the crime did not involve physical harm or violence;
- If the crime did not involve damage to property.

To summarize, an applicant is more likely to obtain a TRP if they have few offences on their record (the fewer the better), the offences were not serious in nature, and some time has passed since the completion of the sentence (including the payment of fines). Additionally, offences that are unrelated to drugs, sex, or weapons lead to a higher likelihood of success in obtaining a TRP.

C. Duration and Limitations

TRPs are issued for a specified amount of time, with a maximum validity of three years. In issuing the permit, an officer will consider the reason for travel; for instance, if an applicant is applying in order to attend a three-day conference, they will usually be issued a three-day TRP. TRPs are valid according to the "Expiry date" or the "Permit in force until date" written on the permit. However, individuals who are traveling to Canada for a specific occasion, such as a wedding or a conference, should expect to be issued a more limited permit.

Generally, permit holders:

- Must comply with the conditions imposed on your TRP;
- Must not work or study without a work or study permit;
- Cannot re-enter Canada without prior authorization;
- Must leave Canada at the end of their authorized period of stay.

D. Frequent Travelers & Multiple Entry

A multiple entry TRP allows the permit holder to enter and leave Canada an indefinite amount of times while their permit is valid. This is a useful option for individuals who must cross the border frequently for work. The reasons for requiring a multiple entry visa should be indicated in the application.

Multiple-entry TRPs are most likely to be issued to people who frequently travel for work, such as flight attendants and pilots, sales representatives, and traveling performers **who can prove their ongoing need to enter Canada**. For instance, a pilot may need to supply IRCC with their work schedule, while a musician may need to furnish a copy of their tour dates.

Failing to respect the conditions of a TRP will further affect an individual's ability to re-enter or remain in Canada. However, the inverse is also true; compliance and proof of good behavior in Canada may make it easier to obtain additional TRPs in the future. Importantly, TRPs solely apply to the ability to enter and remain in Canada. In order to work or study in Canada, individuals are required to apply for a valid work or study permit.

E. Applying for a TRP

Individuals can apply for a TRP at a Canadian visa office, consulate, a port of entry (POE), or with assistance from a Canadian immigration law firm.

Before applying for a TRP, individuals should ensure that there is sufficient time remaining on their passport to cover the period of time they are seeking to remain in Canada. As a valid passport is required for TRP issuance, a TRP cannot be valid for a period extending past the validity of the passport.

As of 2018, the application fee for a TRP is $200.00 (CAN).[2]

As of 2018 the average processing time is four to six (4–6) months if done in advance through a consulate. Applications at the border are approved or denied immediately; however, as demonstrated below, they are riskier.

1. Applying at a port of entry

In order to ensure the best possible outcome on their application, individuals' should be aware of the various pros and cons of applying at different ports of entry. In all, it is easier to obtain a TRP for pleasure or vacation at a POE than at a visa or consular office. Additionally, the presence of kids or elderly parents will often increase the likelihood of success at a POE.

Disclaimer: These are practical tips, based on my professional experience. There is no difference in law between applications made at airport, land border, or seaport.

A) Airport

Those who are confident with their application should attempt to enter via a large, international airport. Large, international airports often have the most experienced officers and there are often advisors that are very knowledgeable on immigration policies. Conversely, smaller airports may not have as experienced officers who are well versed in the necessary policy considerations.

2.   As of June 2015.

Additionally, it is worth noting that if an officer refuses a TRP application, they must accompany the applicant to buy a return ticket to their country of origin and wait with them until they board the aircraft. This may benefit the applicant, as the process is incredibly time consuming for the officer. Therefore, it may be prudent for individuals with strong applications to submit their TRP applications at the airport.

B) Land

It is extremely easy for a border agent to turn a car around at a land border, especially because it takes up very little of their time or resources.

Remote border crossings will likely not have a supervisor, which is a requirement for the approval of a TRP application. As such, even if the application is not rejected outright, the applicant may be made to wait several hours for a supervisor to come in from another border crossing.

Since land-border crossings are particularly fickle, it is not advisable for applicants attempting to cross into Canada via a land border to pre-pay for accommodation or services for their trip to Canada before they are confident that their TRP application is accepted.

C) Sea

Entering Canada by sea can be tricky. Agents at a secluded port may not check to ensure that individuals are not criminally inadmissible to Canada.

However, large ships (including cruise ships) are required to send passenger manifestos to ports ahead of time, so a diligent officer may find someone inadmissible before you even disembark. Those who are passing through Canadian waters on a ship—such as a cruise from the Pacific Northwest to Alaska—must have the proper documentation to receive a TRP in case a Canadian border agent decides to board the ship.

Sea travel is often coupled with air travel. To get onto or off a ship, issuing a TRP may be easier than refusing someone entry, especially if entry is simply to board a ship and leave the country. Basically, the less time spent in Canada, the better. So, if the inadmissible person is leaving Canada on the ship or leaving Canada via an airport the day the cruise starts or ends—there is a high likelihood that a TRP will be issued.

The following table clarifies that major differences between the three types of ports:

POE	Likelihood of Offence Detected	Likelihood of TRP Issuance
Air	Highest	High
Land	Low	Medium
Sea	High	Medium

F. TRP Renewals

Individuals may apply for a new TRP upon the expiration of their current permit. Inadmissible persons must continue to reapply for TRPs in order to enter Canada until they are rehabilitated.

Applying From Within Canada: If the TRP is still valid, the applicant may apply for another TRP from within Canada, provided that they apply at least 30 days before the expiry date. Temporary status is considered "implied" as long as the application was received before the expiry of the current TRP. This means that the applicant may remain in Canada while their permit is being processed. However, the applicant will not be able to leave and re-enter Canada until a new TRP is issued. Additionally, if the TRP is denied, then the applicant must immediately leave the country.

Applying From Outside of Canada: A TRP cannot be extended from outside of Canada. If your TRP has expired and you are outside of the country, you must complete a new application at a consulate or port of entry. Status is not implied, meaning that an individual cannot enter Canada from abroad while their TRP is being processed; they must wait until a decision is rendered before attempting to re-enter Canada.

5.3 Rehabilitation (For Convictions Outside of Canada)

Rehabilitation is a process by which an individual can permanently overcome their inadmissibility. Once an individual has been successfully rehabilitated, their offences will effectively be removed from their criminal record and they will no longer be inadmissible to Canada. In effect, rehabilitation provides them with a "clean slate." Rehabilitation is advisable for those who wish to return repeatedly to Canada.

The rehabilitation process only applies to those who have committed offences outside of Canada.

There are two subsections of Rehabilitation: **Deemed Rehabilitation** and **Criminal Rehabilitation**.

A. Deemed Rehabilitation

An individual who has been convicted of one (1) non-serious offence and more than ten (10) years have passed since the completion of their sentence, may be deemed rehabilitated according to section 18 of *IRPR*. This means that their crime may no longer bar them from entering Canada and they will not require criminal rehabilitation.

It is very important to remember that due to the legislative change in December 2018 upgrading DUI and dangerous driving offences to serious criminality means that anyone who committed an offence of this nature post December 18, 2018 will never be able to be deemed rehabilitated for the offence, even if it is the only conviction they ever receive in their lifetime. An application for Criminal Rehabilitation will always be required to overcome inadmissibility.

Time elapsed since the completion of sentence is the ONLY consideration for deemed rehabilitation. No other factors are considered other than the requisite passage of time.

An individual may be deemed rehabilitated if:

- They have been convicted of only one (1) non-serious offence outside of Canada;
- Ten (10) years have passed since the date that their sentence was completed;
- The offence would not be considered a serious offence under Canadian law[3];
- **OR**
- If they have two (2) offences on their record that are considered to be very minor (the equivalent of summary offences);
- Five (5) years have passed since the date that their sentence was completed.

In all cases, you may only deemed rehabilitated if the crime committed outside Canada has a maximum prison term of less than 10 years if committed in Canada.

If less than ten (10) years have elapsed since the completion of your sentence or you have more than one conviction on your record, you are required to apply for Criminal Rehabilitation in order to become admissible to Canada.

---

3.   See *Chapter Two, Section 2.3 Serious v. Non-Serious Criminality*, p. 18

Offence	Deemed Rehabilitated after Sentence Completion
Equivalent of an indictable offence punishable by <10 years' imprisonment	10 years
Equivalent of an indictable offence punishable by >10 years' imprisonment	Never—must always apply for Criminal Rehabilitation
Equivalent of more than one (1) indictable offence <10 years	Never—must always apply for Criminal Rehabilitation
Equivalent of one (1) indictable offence and one (1) summary offence	Never—must always apply for Criminal Rehabilitation
Equivalent of two or more summary offences	Five (5) years
Equivalent of one summary offence	Not inadmissible, no need for rehabilitation

Deemed Rehabilitation is **not available** when:

- The prescribed period of time has not elapsed.
- The person has committed one indictable offence, and then a subsequent offence of *any* nature.
- The person was deemed rehabilitated and then committed a subsequent offence (removes the application of deemed rehabilitation provisions for any earlier offences).
- The offence under A36 (2)(b) is also described in A36 (1)(b).

1. Confirming deemed rehabilitated

There is no application for deemed rehabilitation, but individuals should be sure that they qualify before trying to enter the country, otherwise, they may be found inadmissible at the border and subsequently denied entry. Deemed rehabilitation can be **assessed free of charge at a Canadian embassy, high commission, or consulate.**

Note: If you **live in the U.S.,** Canadian visa offices in the U.S. do not use this process and applications for deemed rehabilitation are only assessed at a port of entry. However, if you wish to have a finding of rehabilitation completed by the consulate, there is nothing to prevent you from applying for rehabilitation, knowing you are deemed rehabilitated. A standard processing fee ($200.00 CAD) will apply.

B. Criminal Rehabilitation

Criminal Rehabilitation is a process whereby a person requests absolution from the Government of Canada for a particular crime or crimes committed in a foreign country. Rehabilitation means that the individual is considered unlikely to commit new crimes.

In order to be eligible for Criminal Rehabilitation, three (3) criteria must be met:

1) The offence must have been committed outside of Canada and be considered an offence under Canadian criminal law[4].
2) The applicant must have been convicted of, or admitted to committing, the act.
3) Five (5) years must have passed since the full sentence was completed. This means that five years must have passed since **the end** of your prison term, probation, or payment of fines.

Offence	Eligible to Apply for Rehabilitation after Sentence Completion
Equivalent of indictable offence punishable by <10 years' imprisonment	Five years
Equivalent of indictable offence punishable by >10 years' imprisonment	Five years
Equivalent of two or more summary offences	Automatically deemed rehabilitated five years after sentence completion
Equivalent to one summary offence*	Not inadmissible, no need for rehabilitation
Charged but not convicted*	Not inadmissible, no need for rehabilitation

While a summary conviction or a charge, absent a conviction, do not lead to inadmissibility, it is recommended that a person with a charge that appears on their criminal record have the charge explained with a

4.   For more information on determining equivalency, please see Chapter Two.

legal opinion letter. The purpose of this letter is to explain why under Canadian immigration law the individual is not criminally inadmissible to Canada. Border officers are not lawyers and sometimes it is not evident that a person is no longer (or was never) inadmissible to Canada. The more information and explanations that can be presented to them, the higher the likeliness of success.

C. Serious v. Non-Serious Criminality

The process for applying for Criminal Rehabilitation is the same whether or not the offence constitutes serious or non-serious criminality. However, the classification of the offence has the following impacts:

	Deemed rehabilitation available?	Processing Fees	Processing Time	Likelihood of Success
Non-Serious Criminality	Yes. Can be deemed rehabilitated by the passage of time (see above)	$200.00	Faster than below	Relatively likely (where there is only one offence)
Serious Criminality (Maximum prison sentence 10 years or more)	No. Can never be deemed rehabilitated	$1,000.00	Slower than above, since they must be approved by the program manager	Highly discretionary and subjective

D. Calculating the Five (5) Year Waiting Period

The following table explains how to determine the eligibility date for the five (5) year waiting period for different types of sentences.[5]

Suspended sentence	Count five (5) years from the date of sentencing.
Suspended sentence with a fine	Count five (5) years from the date the fine was paid. In the case of varying payment dates, the rehabilitation period starts on the date of the last payment.

---

5.   From IRCC website.

Imprisonment without parole	Count five (5) years from the end of the term of imprisonment.
Imprisonment and parole	Count five (5) years from the completion of parole.
Probation	Probation is part of the sentence. Count five (5) years from the end of the probation period.
Driving probation	Count five (5) years from the end date of the prohibition. You are prohibited from driving.

E. Applying for Rehabilitation

Applications for Criminal Rehabilitation can be made at a **visa office** or **port of entry**.

1. Visa office

Applications are subject to a $200.00 CAD processing fee. An officer will review the application and may ask to see additional documents or call the applicant in for an interview before making a decision.

2. Port of entry

While applications for rehabilitation are technically allowed at POEs, **most POEs refuse to process these applications** due to lack of resources. As such, it is advisable to apply at a visa office prior to travel to avoid disappointment at the border.

3. Factors supporting

Things that may be considered by the officer include:

- How many crimes the individual has committed,
- The circumstances and seriousness of each crime,
- The applicant's behavior since committing the crime,
   → The applicant should demonstrate how they have changed.
- The applicant's explanation of the crimes,
- Whether they are a danger to Canadian society,
   → The applicant should demonstrate that they are highly unlikely to reoffend.
- What support the applicant received from their community,

→ The applicant should demonstrate professional and personal ties, as well as community involvement.

- The applicant's present situation and circumstances.
  → The applicant should demonstrate that they are in a stable condition.
  → The applicant should demonstrate that they are unlikely to reoffend.

F. Supporting Documents

The applicant is required to submit documentation in support of the above factors. Please note that the following is a non-exhaustive list. These are the required documents, but additional documents are recommended to prove the above listed factors. For instance, to have the best chance at success the applicant would provide documentation that substantiates lifestyle changes and their commitment to the health and safety of their community. Applications should be as detailed as possible, and it is common for submitted applications to be in excess of 50 pages.

Forms	Photocopies	Originals
Application for Criminal Rehabilitation	Passport pages that show the applicant's name, date of birth, and country of birth	Criminal clearance from authorities in all countries where they have lived for more than six (6) consecutive months since the age of 18
Use of a Representative (if applicable)	Each court judgement made against them, clearly indicating the charges, verdict, and sentence	If from the U.S., criminal clearance from each state where they have lived for more than six (6) months
Fee for Approval of Application	Copy of the law under which they were convicted	If a juvenile offender, a letter indicating that the country where they were committed has special measures for juveniles

Forms	Photocopies	Originals
	Any other documents relating to sentence, parole, probation, or pardon	

G. Pending Rehabilitation Applications and Inadmissibility

A pending rehabilitation application does not prevent an officer from making a finding of inadmissibility. No provision is made in the *IRPA* or the Regulations to forestall the assessment of criminal inadmissibility when a rehabilitation application is pending.[6] Paragraph 36(3)(c) IRPA is remedial in nature, there is no basis to postpone assessing inadmissibility until the rehabilitation application is assessed.[7] In fact, as the court explicitly stated in *Alabi*:

> It would be inconsistent with the language used in paragraph 36(3)(c) if a finding of criminal inadmissibility – is the normal course – be postponed pending a potential favourable finding on rehabilitation made on the basis of onerous criteria which may not be met.[8]

A pending application does not allow the individual to enter Canada and they are required to await the approval of their application prior entry.

The onus is on the applicant to adduce the evidence establishing that they are deemed rehabilitated.[9]

5.4 Record Suspensions (For Canadian Convictions)

A Record Suspension (formerly known as a pardon) is **a permanent solution to inadmissibility**. It is available to *those who were convicted in Canada*.

A record suspension allows people who were convicted of a criminal offence, but have completed their sentence and demonstrated they are law-abiding citizens for a prescribed number of years, to have their criminal record kept separate and apart from other criminal records. Under the *Criminal Records Act* (CRA), the Parole Board of Canada (PBC) may order, refuse to order, or revoke record suspensions for convictions under federal acts or regulations of Canada.

A record suspension does not erase a conviction from an individual's crimi-

---

6. *Akanmu Alabi v. Canada (Public Safety and Emergency Preparedness)* 2008 FC 370 (CanLII) at 41, see also *Chiarelli*.
7. *Alabi* at 45, affirmed in *Julien v. Canada (Public Safety and Emergency Preparedness)* 2015 FC 150 (CanLII).
8. *Alabi*, at 46.
9. *Alabi*, throughout.

nal history. Instead, it sets the conviction aside from the rest of the individual's criminal record.

If you received a record suspension or a discharge for your *conviction in another country*, **the pardon may not be valid in Canada and you may still be inadmissible.**

A. Eligibility

A person is eligible for a record suspension if:

1) Five (5) years have passed after the completion* of a sentence for a summary offence
2) Ten (10) years have passed after the completion of a sentence for one, non-serious indictable offence

*An individual is deemed to have completed a sentence if:

- They have paid all fines, surcharges, costs, restitution and compensation orders in full;
- They have served all sentences of imprisonment, conditional sentences, including parole and statutory release;
- They have satisfied their probation order(s).

*A person is **ineligible** for a record suspension if they have been convicted of:*

1) A *Schedule 1* Offence (sexual offence involving a child) under the Criminal Records Act, or
2) More than three (3) offences prosecuted by indictment each with a prison sentence of two (2) years or more.

B. Applying for a Record Suspension

Unlike TRPs and criminal rehabilitation, record suspensions are not under the jurisdiction of IRCC. Rather, record suspensions are granted by the Parole Board of Canada (PBC). Applications are made through their website. The PBC charges $631 to process a record suspension application. In 2016-2017, the PBC granted 8,191 record suspensions with a grant rate of 71%.[10]

---

10. https://www.canada.ca/en/parole-board/corporate/transparency/reporting-to-canadians/record-suspension-report-to-parliament-2016-2017.html#d2

C. Absolute or Conditional Discharge

Individuals who received a conditional discharge, absolute discharge, dismissal, or any other non-conviction *do not* need to apply for a record suspension. A person does not need to apply for a record suspension if their criminal record consists *only* of absolute or conditional discharges.

All discharges handed down by the court on or after July 24, 1992 will automatically be removed from the CPIC computer system one (1) year (absolute discharge) or three (3) years (conditional discharge) after the court decision.[11]

D. Revocation of a Record Suspension

*The PBC may **revoke** a record suspension if:*

- The person is later convicted of a summary offence under a federal act or regulation of Canada;
- The PBC finds that the person is no longer of good conduct;
- The PBC learns that a false or deceptive statement was made, or relevant information was concealed at the time of the application.

*A Record Suspension may **cease to have effect** if:*

- The person is subsequently convicted of an indictable offence under a federal act or regulation of Canada;
- The person is convicted of an offence punishable either on indictable or summary conviction;
- If the PBC is convinced by new information that the person was not actually eligible for a record suspension at the time it was ordered.

In the above-mentioned circumstances, the records of the offences will again be kept with the other conviction records.

5.5 Convictions Inside and Outside of Canada

In order to overcome inadmissibility, individuals with convictions both inside and outside of Canada will need to apply for Criminal Rehabilitation or a TRP (to rectify the foreign conviction) and a record suspension (to rectify the Canadian conviction).

---

11.   IRCC website;

Chapter 6

Misrepresentation

Withholding documents, or sending false information or documents to IRCC is a serious offence. It is a type of fraud, and it is called misrepresentation. The law does not differentiate between direct or indirect, deliberate or non-deliberate misrepresentations—they are all considered equally fraudulent.[1] Per s. 40 of the *IRPA*, misrepresentation will lead to inadmissibility to, or removal from, Canada. Subsequently, the individual will be inadmissible to Canada for a period of five years.

40. (1) A permanent resident or a foreign national is inadmissible for misrepresentation

- o   (*a*) for directly or indirectly misrepresenting or withholding material facts relating to a relevant matter that induces or could induce an error in the administration of this Act;

---

1.   *Wang v. Canada (Citizenship and Immigration)*, 2015 FC 647 at para 24, clearly stated in s. 40 IRPA etc. Wang further clarifies that even indirect misrepresentation by a third party constitutes misrepresentation for the purposes of s.40.

    o   (*b*) for being or having been sponsored by a person who is determined to be inadmissible for misrepresentation;

    o   (*c*) on a final determination to vacate a decision to allow their claim for refugee protection or application for protection; or

    o   (*d*) on ceasing to be a citizen under paragraph 10(1)(*a*) of the *Citizenship Act*, in the circumstances set out in subsection 10(2) of that Act.

(2) The following provisions govern subsection (1):

    o   (*a*) the permanent resident or the foreign national continues to be inadmissible for misrepresentation for a period of five years following, in the case of a determination outside Canada, a final determination of inadmissibility under subsection (1) or, in the case of a determination in Canada, the date the removal order is enforced; and

    o   (*b*) paragraph (1)(*b*) does not apply unless the Minister is satisfied that the facts of the case justify the inadmissibility.

(3) A foreign national who is inadmissible under this section may not apply for permanent resident status during the period referred to in paragraph (2)(*a*).[2]

Again, the *IRPA* does not distinguish between deliberate and innocent misrepresentations, including those made on faulty legal advice.[3]

6.1 Defining Misrepresentation

Misrepresentation is defined as "an assertion that does not accord with the facts" and "the act of making a false or misleading assertion about something with the intent to deceive. The word denotes not just written or spoken words, but also any other conduct that amount to a false assertion."[4] Misrepresentation may sometimes be referred to as "false pretenses." The *Act* and *Regulations* do not create a distinction between deliberate misrepresentations and innocent misrepresentations, including those made on faulty legal advice.

There are several different forms of misrepresentation, including:

---

2.   *Immigration and Refugee Protection Act*, Canada 2014, c 4, s 40 [IRPA].
3.   *Chen v. Canada (Citizenship and Immigration)*, 2005 FC 678 at 10, [2005] FCJ No 852 (QL).
4.   Black's Law Dictionary.

Fraudulent Misrepresentation	"A false statement that is known to be false or is made recklessly – without knowing or caring whether it is true or false – and that is intended to induce a party to detrimentally rely on it."
Negligent Misrepresentation	"A careless or inadvertent false statement in circumstances where care should have been taken."
Direct Misrepresentation	Situations where the person makes a misrepresentation or withholds information themselves—on their own behalf.
Indirect Misrepresentation	Where a third party makes a misrepresentation or withholds information.
Withholding	"To hold back from doing or taking an action; to keep (within); to refrain from granting, giving, allowing or "letting 'it' be known." People can misrepresent themselves by being silent just as easily as a person who actively states a "mistruth." A person who refuses or declines to answer a question, preferring instead to allow outdated or false information to be accepted as current or true information, is engaging in the activity of misrepresentation.
Material Misrepresentation	Material misrepresentation encompasses document fraud, including altered passports, visas, diplomas, degrees, apprenticeships, trade papers, test results, birth certificates, marriage and divorce papers, or police certificates.

Three principles of misrepresentation emerged from the seminal case of *Minister of Manpower and Immigration v. Brooks* (hereafter *Brooks*). First, that intent to mislead is not necessary, as innocent misrepresentation still constitutes misrepresentation; as Justice Laskin (as he was then) stated, "I cannot be persuaded that intentional or willful deception should be read in as a prerequisite."[5] Second, the information that was misrepresented need not be of the kind or degree that would cause inadmissibility.[6] Third, that misrepresentation is material "simply if it averts or discourages a line of inquiry."[7]

---

5. *Ibid* at 7; *Minister of Manpower and Immigration v. Brooks*, 1974 S.C.R. 850 at 865 [Brooks].
6. *Supra* Gordon at 7; *Supra* Brooks at 873.
7. *Ibid* Brooks at 873; *Supra* Gordon at 7.

All three of the principles derived from *Brooks* help us better define the boundaries of the misrepresentation as they have been applied through the *IRPA*. The first tells us that even innocent misrepresentations count as such, the second tells us that the hidden or warped information does not need to be the reason an applicant would become inadmissible, and the third tells us that misrepresentation becomes material as long as it changes how the *IRPA* is applied to the applicant, or if it changes how a government official would handle their inquiry.

6.2 Direct Misrepresentation, Indirect Misrepresentation, and Withholding

Direct misrepresentation is when the false pretense or misinformation is presented by the individual on their own behalf, while indirect misrepresentation occurs where a third party is present and withholds or misrepresents their information for them.[8] Withholding information is considered to be equivalent to misrepresentation in immigration cases.

To summarize, applicants can misrepresent themselves by not answering a question (withholding), or by giving outdated information (direct misrepresentation); the effects of this behavior are the same regardless of whether this was done orally to an officer or in a written application.

6.3 The Duty to Disclose

One of the positive duties associated with misrepresentation is the duty to disclose. The duty to disclose is "the obligation to provide truthful, complete information in an immigration matter."[9] The duty to disclose is broader than the concept of withholding. An individual withholds information when they decline to answer a question or give a partial answer to a question; the duty to disclose concerns the withholding of information that was not asked. For instance, if the applicant knows that a certain conviction would make them inadmissible to Canada, but they were never asked about possible inadmissibility on an application or in person. This sort of situation may trigger the duty to disclose.

It is difficult to outline the scope of the duty to disclose, as it is often at an official's discretion. However, there are four (4) distinct circumstances where a duty to disclose has been found:

1. When a relevant question is asked;
2. When there is a change of material circumstances;
3. When a statute requires disclosure;

---

8. *Immigration and Refugee Protection Act*, Canada 2014, c 4, s 40 [IRPA]
9. Gordon Maynard, "Misrepresentation: A Historical, Statutory and Judicial Analysis" (2009) National Citizenship and Immigration Law Conference 1 at 2 [Gordon].

4. When the surrounding circumstances require disclosure, even if a question is not asked[10].

Several U.S. states maintain their own record system. Record updates are made at the state level only, so the FBI can only access, not modify, the system. As such, certain criminal convictions may not appear on an FBI record check. An applicant is still under the obligation to disclose any convictions or charges, unless they have been criminally rehabilitated.

The Court defined the scope and rigidity of the duty to disclose in *Mohammed v. Canada (Minister of Citizenship and Immigration)* (hereafter *Mohammed*). Mr. Mohammed was deemed inadmissible under Section 40 of the IRPA because he did not disclose the fact that he was married in between receiving his visa and arriving to Canada. He was found to be under the duty to disclose despite the fact that he did not speak English, was unable to communicate at the port of entry because there was no interpreter, was unable to read any of his immigration documents, was not asked any questions, and had no idea he was under a duty to disclose.[11] Mohammed had applied with his family to come to Canada as a dependent. Coming from a small village in Bangladesh, no one in the family could read, write or speak English. Therefore, Mohammed relied on the only person in his village with knowledge of English, Mr. Alaam, to assist him with the immigration documents. Mr. Alaam allegedly did not explain any of the paperwork to the family while filling out their application.[12]

Despite the fact that there was absolutely no way that Mohammed could have known that he was misrepresenting his marital status, he was still deemed inadmissible to Canada.[13] The court found that despite Mr. Mohammed's assertion that his misrepresentation was an innocent and invincible error, he was still inadmissible because the information on his application was incorrect.[14]

In *Zewdie v. Canada* (hereafter *Zewdie*), the court affirmed that it did not matter whether the applicant could effectively communicate or understand the meaning of the duty to disclose, as the statutory obligation of disclosure overpowers the argument of innocently misrepresenting.[15]

Both of the aforementioned cases rely on the statutory obligation to disclose changes in marital status whilst applying to immigrate to Canada. Essentially, when there is a statutory obligation to disclose, an individual cannot argue innocent misinterpretation, as one should be aware of the laws and regulations gov-

---

10. *Ibid* at 6.
11. *Mohammed v. Canada (Minister of Citizenship and Immigration)*, 1997 3 FCR 299.
12. *Ibid*.
13. *Ibid*.
14. *Ibid*.
15. Canada vs. Zewdie, 2006 I.D.D. No. 22.

erning immigration applications. However, the boundaries of the duty to disclose become are further complicated when there is no statutory duty to disclose, as "one must look at the surrounding circumstances to decide whether the applicant has failed to comply… as applicants cannot be expected to anticipate the kinds of information that immigration officials might be interested in receiving."[16] There is clearly no way that applicants can spontaneously disclose all information, specifically in cases where they are not aware what information is relevant. In these circumstances, the duty to disclose is gauged by an official to determine whether a reasonable person would have known to disclose the information in the given circumstance.[17] An exception arises where applicants can show that they honestly and reasonably believed that they were not withholding material information.[18] If an individual has no subjective knowledge that they are misrepresenting, and statues do not govern the particular circumstance, then the applicant may make an argument for innocent misinterpretation in an attempt to circumvent inadmissibility under Section 40 of *IRPA*.

6.4 The Duty of Candour

As exemplified by the duty to disclose, the Canadian immigration system is a strong self-reporting scheme. The companion to the duty to disclose is the duty of candour. The Courts have held that an applicant owes a duty of candour to disclose material information to the immigration authority.[19] While the duty to disclose dictates when an applicant should present information that may impact the success of their application, the duty of candour outlines *how much* information the applicant should provide. In effect, it requires an applicant to elaborate to the fullest of their ability when asked a question by IRCC. For example, the duty of candour is engaged when a CBSA officer asks about changes in the applicant's marital status since they first applied, and they tell her that they have recently become divorced, but they fail to mention that they have subsequently become engaged. In this scenario, the duty of candour would require the applicant to disclose every change in their marital status, including the engagement.

As illustrated by the preceding example, the duty to disclose and the duty of candour often occur simultaneously, making them difficult to distinguish.

---

16. *Supra* Gordon at 11; Baro v Minister of Citizenship and Immigration, 2007 FC 1299.
17. *Supra* Gordon at 11.
18. *Medel v. Canada (Minister of Employment and Immigration)*, [1990] 2 F.C. 345, [1990] F.C.J. No. 318 (F.C.A.) (QL).
19. *Marin Saldarriaga v. Canada (Citizenship and Immigration)*, 2011 CanLII 28873 (CA IRB), at para 44.

6.5 Document Fraud

Document fraud is a form of material misrepresentation and can involve false or altered documents, such as:

- Passports and travel documents,
- Visas,
- Diplomas, degrees, and apprenticeship or trade papers,
- Birth, marriage, final divorce, trade, or apprenticeship papers, and
- Police certificates.

6.6 Consequences of Misrepresentation

Sending false documents will result in either the refusal of an application, or a more serious penalty, such as:

- Forbidden to enter Canada for at least five years,
- Have a record of fraud with the IRCC,
- Lose your permanent residency,
- Be charged with a crime, or
- Be removed from Canada[20].

6.7 Procedural Fairness and Enforcement

Broadly framed, procedural fairness concerns the entitlement to rights during the deliberation of a file. For immigration purposes, procedural fairness includes processing a file without undue delay, the opportunity for applicants to disabuse officers of any concerns, fettered use of officer discretion, adequate communication with applicants, and decision-making based on the *IRPA* and *IRPR*.[21]

For example, if somebody is being accused of misrepresentation, they should always be given an opportunity to respond to such allegations.[22] Furthermore, applicants must receive fair and equitable treatment, which means that applicants with similar situations should be receiving consistent treatment from officials and have somewhat similar results. Another aspect of procedural fairness is that decisions must be based on the *IRPA* and *IRPR*, and they must be cited in the record of refusal if an application is in fact refused. Applications should also be processed in a timely manner, which means there should not be any undue delays. Applicants should also have all the documentation they need from offi-

---

20. *IRPA* s. 40 (2), (3).
21. http://www.cic.gc.ca/english/resources/manuals/op/op01-eng.pdf
22. Citizenship and Immigration Canada, "Evaluating Inadmissibility" (2013) at 30 [ENF 2].

cials, and all interview or application decision-making should be accurately and responsibly communicated to them, unless something is exempted for security reasons. Procedural fairness is extremely important in order to avoid discrimination, unfair treatment, and unnecessarily long waiting times.

The following table outlines the principles of procedural fairness that an applicant can expect from the treatment of their immigration application.[23]

Principle	Explanation
Communicating adequately and accurately with applicants	• Officers should give applicants adequate notice regarding the process or the interview that will result or lead to a decision. • Officers should accurately describe to applicants the documentation they are required to submit in order to address their concern. • With the exception of information that must be exempted for security reasons, the applicant is entitled to receive and comment on any relevant documents obtained by the officer that will be considered by the decision-maker.
Processing without undue delay	• Officers must show diligence in processing applications. • Visa offices must not appear to frustrate processing through unacceptable delays. • A delay that cannot be justified is a denial of procedural fairness.
Whoever hears, must decide	• "Hear" in this context means that the person with the legal authority to make a decision must do so. • A decision-maker should not indicate that they simply concur with the recommendations of an intermediary. They must indicate that they have weighed all salient factors of the application and have made their own decision on the merits of those factors.

---

23. Per CIC guideline manual (above link).

Principle	Explanation
	• Decision maker must render the decision based on complete information, so all documents provided by the applicant must be forwarded to the decision-maker for consideration (needs primary documentation not just a summary of contents for documentation).
Applicants must have an opportunity to disabuse officers of any concerns	• Applicants must be allowed to bring evidence and to make an argument. This includes being provided with adequate translation services. • The applicant must be made aware of the "case to be met," i.e., the information known by the officer must be made available to the applicant prior to the decision being made. • Officers should give factual and objective reasons for their decision.
Decisions must be based on the *IRPA* and the *IRPR*	• The provision of the Act or Regulations must be cited in the record of refusal. • All communications should direct the reader's attention to the appropriate legislative provision.
Applicants must receive fair and equitable treatment	• Officers must be consistent in the treatment of applicants in similar situations.
Discretion must be properly fettered	• It should be plain to applicants that officers have used their authority to decide freely.

6.8 Responding to Concerns about Misrepresentation

An individual should always be given the opportunity to respond to concerns about a possible misrepresentation. As noted above, officers are required to inform applicants of any issues with their applications and provide them with adequate time to respond. This includes the opportunity to assuage those concerns by providing any supporting documents or testimony proving that all representations were truthful and accurate.

At a visa office: Once the applicant has been given the opportunity to respond to the concerns, the designated officer will render a final decision regarding the misrepresentation. They will subsequently either issue or refuse the application.

At a port of entry or inland: The Minister's delegate will determine whether or not to refer the case to the Immigration and Refugee Board (IRB) for an admissibility hearing. The IRB is an independent administrative tribunal that makes legally binding decisions on issues of immigration.

An Immigration Appeals Division (IAD) Member will decide the appeal at the IRB. Individuals should supply documentation proving that they did not misrepresent information that was important to their immigration application. They will also have the opportunity to respond to allegations raised by the Minister's counsel regarding the CBCA decision. In short, applicants are entitled to:

- Know the case to be met,
- Have an opportunity to present evidence relevant to the case,
- Provide a response to facts or new information that will be considered by the decision-maker, and
- Have their evidence fully and fairly considered.

If the Member decides that there was no misrepresentation, the individual will be allowed to enter or remain in Canada. If they make a finding of misrepresentation or find the individual otherwise inadmissible to Canada, they will issue a removal order to the CBSA.

6.9 Conclusion

As previously stated, the *IRPA* refrains from distinguishing between direct or indirect and innocent or deliberate misrepresentation, which means that all kinds are equally prohibited under the law. Additionally, within misrepresentation, there is also the government's duty to enforce procedural fairness, so that all voices are heard, all facts are considered fairly, and consistency is applied to all similar cases in a timely manner.

To summarize:

Case	Established Legal Principle
Brooks	There are three (3) core principles of contemporary misrepresentation: 1. Intentional deception is not required 2. Misrepresentation does not need to be material 3. Misrepresentation is material as long as it averts or discourages a line of inquiry
Mohammed	Innocent misrepresentation is indistinguishable from intentional misrepresentation.
Zewdie	Statutory duties outweigh the argument of innocent misrepresentation.
Medel	An exception arises where applicants can show that they honestly and reasonably believed that they were not withholding material information

Chapter 7

Representation

All applicants for Canadian immigration, be they citizenship, permanent residency, or temporary entry applicants, are allowed to seek advice on their application. People seek advice from a number of different individuals or organizations, for example, lawyers, citizenship and immigration consultants, friends and family, or NGOs and religious organizations. Applicants can use a legal representative when dealing with Immigration, Refugees, and Citizenship Canada (IRCC), the Immigration and Refugee Board of Canada, and the Canada Border Services Agency (CBSA). These representatives can assemble applications on an individual's behalf, using their legal expertise and familiarity with the system to improve the chances of the applications' approval.

These representatives can be remunerated—such as a Canadian immigration lawyer or immigration consultant, or unpaid—such as a community group or legal clinic. In order to act on an individual's behalf and be eligible to receive information on the file's progress, the third part must submit a copy of the Use of a Representative Form (IMM 5476E) to the appropriate government body. The moment a person receives advice on their file, they are required to fill out IMM 5176E. This applies even in situations where representatives give consultations and do not handle the file any further.

7.1 Unauthorized Representatives

IRCC has developed regulations and guidelines to ensure that only authorized representatives can legally provide guidance for monetary consideration. Bill C-35, *An Act to Amend the Immigration and Refugee Protection Act* and Bill C-24, *the Strengthening Canadian Citizenship Act*, made it an offence for unauthorized individuals to knowingly, directly or indirectly, represent or advise a person in connection with a citizenship or immigration application or proceeding—or offer to do so—for a fee.[1] If an individual who is not authorized to provide representation or advice for consideration under section 91 or section 21.1 of the *IRPA* knowingly does so, they are committing an offence and are liable on conviction to receive a fine or imprisonment, or both. The penalties for unauthorized misrepresentation are outlined below.

7.2 Who is Authorized to Represent?

IRPA dictates that there are five different categories of individuals or bodies that may legally represent or advise an applicant on their immigration application.[2] The first category includes both lawyers and notaries that are in good standing with their respective provincial societies.[3] The second category includes members of said societies who are not lawyers or notaries but are in good standing with the society.[4] The third category discusses students who are studying law, who are said to be permitted to represent as long as they have a lawyer that is supervising them as they work for the applicant.[5] Category four is rather unusual, but includes entities or representatives of certain entities that have been given the right to represent in agreement with Her Majesty.[6] Lastly, designations can be made by the Minister, and those designated can represent or advise a person in regards to their application.[7] If anybody outside of these five categories were to advise or represent, then they would be susceptible to penalties under Section 91 subsection 9.

A. Compensated Representatives

- Members in good standing of a Canadian provincial/territorial law society (i.e. properly accredited Canadian lawyers) (including paralegals).
- Members of the *Chambre des notaires du Quebec*.

---

1. http://www.cic.gc.ca/english/resources/manuals/ip/ip09-eng.pdf at 3.1 and 3.2.
2. *Ibid* at s 91 (2)-(5)
3. *Ibid* at s 91 (2)(a)
4. *Ibid* at s 91 (2)(b)
5. *Ibid* at s 91 (3)
6. *Ibid* at s 91 (4)
7. *Ibid* at s 91 (5)

- Members of the Immigration Consultants of Canada Regulatory Council (ICCRC).
- Students-at-law under direct supervision of a lawyer or notary.

Each of the aforementioned institutions has online directories. Consultant fraud is a common occurrence, thus it is advised that an individual check to make sure that their representative is properly accredited before engaging their services.

B. Uncompensated Representatives

- Family or friends.
- NGOs.
- Religious organizations.
- Community groups.
- Pro-bono legal clinics.

The following tables provides clarification of the various categories of representatives[8]:

Compensated Representatives	Individuals who receive some form of consideration (typically in the form of a fee or payment) for the provision of advice or representation to someone in connection with citizenship or immigration matters.
Authorized Representatives	Individuals who are members in good standing of a Canadian provincial/territorial law society—including paralegals—the *Chambre des notaires du Québec*, or the Immigration Consultants of Canada Regulatory Council (ICCRC).
Uncompensated Representatives	Any person who does not receive direct or indirect consideration for providing advice or representation on citizenship or immigration matters. This could include a family member, friend, or a member of an international, religious or non-governmental organization.

---

8.   Taken from http://www.cic.gc.ca/english/resources/manuals/ip/ip09-eng.pdf (table 4).

Unauthorized Representatives	Individuals who receive some form of consideration for advising or representing a client on citizenship or immigration matters and who are **not** members of a Canadian provincial/territorial law society—including paralegals—the *Chambre des notaires du Québec* or the Immigration Consultants of Canada Regulatory Council (ICCRC).

7.3 Penalty for unauthorized representatives

Unauthorized representatives can only collect documents for an immigration application, are not allowed to provide counsel on the means of submitting said application or to provide advice on how the applicant should try to enter Canada. If an unauthorized representative is paid for counsel on the immigration application process, then they could be convicted of an indictable or summary offence, making this action a hybrid crime.[9] Since the amendments made in 2011, in Bill C-35 *An Act to Amend the IRPA*, unlawful representation can be punished by

1. Indictment: with a maximum fine of $100,000, or a prison term of no more than 2 years, or both,
2. Summary: with a maximum fine of $20,000, or a prison term of no more than 6 months, or both.[10]

These amendments raised the stakes, in an attempt to deter applicants from using unauthorized representatives, and to deter unqualified third parties from dispensing false information and making a profit of misleading clients. If an applicant cannot access an authorized representative, they can have unpaid third parties act on their behalf as long as they are family members, friends, non-profit groups or religious groups. They can also have the U.S. criminal lawyer who represented them in criminal cases assist them with their application, as long as they are acting *pro bono*. Should any of these individuals or groups receive payment or consideration however, then they would become a part of the unauthorized representative category and their penalty would be decided accordingly. It is important to note that while the attorney who handled the criminal case in the jurisdiction here the offence occurred may be the most familiar with the facts of the case, they cannot handle the immigration documentation unless they are accredited by one of the aforementioned Canadian organizations.

The major portions of Section 91 of the *IRPA* are reproduced below.

---

9.   *Ibid* at s 91 (9)
10. *Ibid* at s 91 (9) (a) - (b)

Representation or Advice

Representation or advice for consideration
91. (1) Subject to this section, no person shall knowingly, directly or indirectly, represent or advise a person for consideration — or offer to do so — in connection with the submission of an expression of interest under subsection 10.1(3) or a proceeding or application under this Act.

Persons who may represent or advise
2) A person does not contravene subsection (1) if they are
   (*a*) a lawyer who is a member in good standing of a law society of a province or a notary who is a member in good standing of the Chambre des notaires du Québec;
   (*b*) any other member in good standing of a law society of a province or the Chambre des notaires du Québec, including a paralegal; or
   (*c*) a member in good standing of a body designated under subsection (5).

Students-at-law
(3) A student-at-law does not contravene subsection (1) by offering or providing representation or advice to a person if the student-at-law is acting under the supervision of a person mentioned in paragraph (2)(a) who is representing or advising the person — or offering to do so — in connection with the submission of an expression of interest under subsection 10.1(3) or a proceeding or application under this Act.

Agreement or arrangement with Her Majesty
(4) An entity, including a person acting on its behalf, that offers or provides services to assist persons in connection with the submission of an expression of interest under subsection 10.1(3) or an application under this Act, including for a permanent or temporary resident visa, travel documents or a work or study permit, does not contravene subsection (1) if it is acting in accordance with an agreement or arrangement between that entity and Her Majesty in right of Canada that authorizes it to provide those services.

Designation by Minister

(5) The Minister may, by regulation, designate a body whose members in good standing may represent or advise a person for consideration — or offer to do so — in connection with the submission of an expression of interest under subsection 10.1(3) or a proceeding or application under this Act.

Penalties

(9) Every person who contravenes subsection (1) commits an offence and is liable

(*a*) on conviction on indictment, to a fine of not more than $100,000 or to imprisonment for a term of not more than two years, or to both; or

(*b*) on summary conviction, to a fine of not more than $20,000 or to imprisonment for a term of not more than six months, or to both.

Appendix A

Index of Terms and Abbreviations

Table of Abbreviations

ARC	Authorization to Return to Canada
CBSA	Canadian Border Services Agency
CPIC	Canada Police Information Centre
CRA	Criminal Records Act
DUI	Driving Under the Influence
IRB	Immigration and Refugee Board
IRCC	Immigration, Refugees, and Citizenship Canada
IRPA	Immigration and Refugee Protection Act
IRPR	Immigration and Refugee Protection Regulations
NCIC	National Crime Information Center
PDP	Previously Deported Person
PBC	Parole Board of Canada
POA	Provincial Offences Act
POE	Port of Entry
TRP	Temporary Resident Permit

Index of Terms

Act of Parliament

An Act of Parliament is a statute enacted as primary legislation by the Canadian government. A Canadian Act of Parliament is a federal bill which has been passed by the House of Commons and the Senate, received Royal Assent and been proclaimed. In Canada, criminal law and immigration law are under federal jurisdiction. As such, all acts pertaining to immigration and criminal justice are Acts of Parliament. For the purposes of criminal inadmissibility, the primary acts are the Criminal Code of Canada and the Immigration and Refugee Protection Act. Other relevant acts include: Youth Criminal Justice Act, Controlled Drugs and Substances Act, and Canadian Anti-Terrorism Act.

Certificate of Departure

This document confirms that the person named on the removal order has appeared before an officer at the port of entry to verify their departure, will depart from Canada, and has been authorized to enter their country of destination. This document also confirms the enforcement of a removal order outside Canada. This certificate is conferred by a POE officer, a removal officer, or an officer at a Canadian visa office to a foreign national who is the subject of an enforceable removal order.

Conditional Discharge

A conditional discharge is a sentence passed in criminal court in which an individual is found guilty of an offence but is deemed not to have been convicted after serving a period of probation. A court may grant a conditional or absolute discharge only for offences with no minimum penalty, and a maximum penalty of less than fourteen years. Though not a conviction, the offender has to fulfill certain conditions, such as probation. If the conditions are not met, the offender must return to court to be convicted; if the conditions are met, the conditional discharge become an absolute discharge and the offence will not appear on a criminal record check. Conditional and absolute discharges are prescribed by s. 730 of the *Criminal Code*.

Drug Detection and THC

Delta-9-tetrahydrocannabinol (THC) is a cannabinoid; an active chemical ingredient produced by the cannabis plant which is known to cause the psychoactive effects felt from its intake. With the amendments made to the *Criminal Code* due to Bill C-46, Canadian police are now trained to detect if you are driving under the influence of a drug and enforce drug-impaired driving laws using the Standard Field Sobriety Test (SFST) and Drug Recognition Expert (DRE). Additionally, police are now equipped with drug screening devices, and are permitted to conduct legal roadside testing in order to detect for the recent presence of several drugs, including THC from cannabis, cocaine, and methamphetamine. If police suspect driving inhibition due to a drug, they can demand an oral fluid sample and/or conduct an SFST.

Hybrid Offence
Term applied to a criminal offence that may be tried by summary conviction procedure or by indictment at the option of the prosecutor. A hybrid offence is considered an indictable offence until the Crown elects to proceed by way of summary conviction. The majority of offences in the *Criminal Code* are hybrid offences.

Illicit Cannabis
Cannabis not purchased from a provincially-licensed retailer, or online from federally-licensed producers. Original packaging and receipts can be used as proof of licit purchase.

Indictable Offence
An indictable offence is a criminal offence which is triable by way of indictment. The most serious criminal offences—for example, murder—are indictable offences. Some offences may be tried summarily or by way of indictment (see: Hybrid Offences).

Onus
The onus dictates who bears the burden of proof. Generally, the onus is on the Minister to adduce sufficient evidence to establish the alleged grounds of inadmissibility. On appeal of refusal order, the burden shifts to the applicant.

Procedural Fairness
Procedural fairness represents a safeguard on administrative decision-making. Procedural fairness requires that a complainant be provided with an opportunity to make submissions before any action is taken on the basis of a report. In order to ensure that such submissions are made on an informed basis, the complainant to be informed of the substance of the case against them.

Removal Order

Removal orders are issued by IRCC or CBSA to foreign nationals who are not authorized to enter or remain in Canada. There are three types of removal orders: departure orders, exclusion orders, and deportation orders.

Departure Order: requires the individual to leave Canada within 30 days and obtain a Certificate of Departure. If an individual complies with this order they may re-enter Canada without additional documentation in the future. If they do not comply they will be subject to a Deportation Order.

Exclusion Order: requires an individual to leave Canada and obtain a Certificate of Departure detailing the date that they left Canada. If 12 months have passed since they have left Canada, they may re-enter the country without obtaining any additional documentation. If they wish to re-enter before the allotted time (or if they were not issued a Certificate of Departure) then they must apply for an Authorization to Return to Canada.

Deportation Order: requires an individual to leave Canada by the date indicated on the order. In order to re-enter Canada at any time after being deported, they must apply for Authorization to Return to Canada.

Standards of Proof

Beyond a Reasonable Doubt is the *criminal standard* of proof. This is the strictest possible standard of proof. Beyond a Reasonable Doubt is not a standard used in Canadian immigration law.

Balance of Probabilities is the civil standard of proof for questions of law. It is the standard used for most administrative tribunals. It means that the evidence presented must show that the facts as alleged are **more probable than not**. Accordingly, a party having the burden of proof by a "balance of probabilities" must be able to persuade that the evidence presented outweighs opposing evidence. "Balance of probabilities" is a higher standard of proof than "reasonable grounds to believe," but is lower than the criminal standard of "beyond a reasonable doubt" used in criminal proceedings.

Section 36(3)(d) of the *IRPA* states that a determination of whether a permanent resident has committed an act described in paragraph (1)(c) must be based on a balance of probabilities. *Questions of law* are decided on the balance of probabilities and are reviewed on the *correctness standard.*

Reasonable Grounds to Believe is the standard of proof for *questions of fact*, i.e. the findings of fact made by a tribunal. Unless otherwise provided, inadmissibility may be based on facts for which there are reasonable grounds to believe that they have occurred, are occurring, or may occur.

The Supreme Court has stated that the "reasonable grounds to believe" standard requires something more than mere suspicion, but less than the standard applicable in civil matters of proof on the balance of probabilities. In essence, reasonable grounds will exist where there is an objective basis for the belief which is based on compelling and credible information.

In the case of a foreign national, an officer must be satisfied that there are "reasonable grounds to believe" that an act has occurred. As previously noted, permanent residents will be assessed by the high "balance of probabilities" standard.

Summary Conviction Offence

A summary conviction is an offence that is tried summarily. Less-serious criminal offences are typically classified as summary conviction offences. Some offences are hybrid offences and can be tried by either summary or indictment, depending on the prosecutor's election.

Appendix B

Case Studies

The following case studies are based on real files handled by our office. They demonstrate the outcomes of different applications in various circumstances. I have included my analysis in order to highlight the factors that likely affected the outcome of the application.

Client 1

Type of Application	Criminal Rehabilitation
Offence	Homicide by vehicle (per Pennsylvania Statutes s. 3732)
Facts	In May 1998, client crashed into an oncoming car while trying to pass another vehicle in a narrowed construction area. He was neither speeding nor impaired. The driver of the other vehicle succumbed to his injuries.
Canadian Equivalent	s. 294(4) *Criminal Code*: "Dangerous Operation Causing Death."
Reason for Travel	Humanitarian and compassionate grounds • Wife's family live in Ontario. • Couple had a baby, which caused the wife more stress during travel and required the client to accompany her on visits. • Wished to attend family events in Canada, including: brother's high school graduation, cousin's wedding, and to visit a terminally ill uncle.
Outcome	APPROVED
Analysis	This application was likely approved because a sufficient amount of time has passed between the offence and the application for rehabilitation. Though a person was killed during the incident, the applicant did not demonstrate any type of risky behavior, he was not driving too quickly or impaired. The applicant has strong ties to Canada, through his wife and there is compassionate reason to allow the applicant into Canada.

Client 2

Type of Application	Criminal Rehabilitation
Offence	Possession with intent to deliver LSD (*per* Wisconsin Code 161.41)
Facts	In 1982, the client delivered a bag containing 4,000 LSD tablets to an associate who then tried to sell them to an undercover police officer. He was sentenced to 36 months of probation and discharged after 21 months, in addition to being fined.
Canadian Equivalent	Controlled Drugs and Substances Act s. 5(1): Trafficking in substance
Reason for Travel	Leisure • Wants to travel with his grandchildren or attend a conference.
Outcome	REFUSED
Analysis	In my opinion, this application had a strong likelihood to be accepted. For one, he was convicted over 30 years ago for a non-violent offence that did not result in any bodily injury. He has significantly rehabilitated himself since the offence—quickly finding employment and remaining gainfully employed ever since. Since serving his sentence, he has become a leader in his field and an active member of his community. His application includes multiple glowing references from esteemed friends and colleagues attesting to his good character. Nonetheless, the officer came to a different conclusion, which demonstrates the role of the officer's discretion in processing these types of applications.

Client 3

Type of Application	Criminal rehabilitation and TRP
Offence	Conspiracy to manufacture a controlled substance (per United States Code 846 & 841(a)(1))
Facts	In June 1981, client asked to create a formula and obtain equipment to manufacture meth. Client was sentenced to 36 months probation for "conspiracy to manufacture a controlled substance," the Canadian equivalent being s. 7 *Controlled Drugs and Substances Act.*
Canadian Equivalent	s. 7 *Controlled Drugs and Substances Act*
Reason for Travel	Business • Client's company had a contract with a Canadian company. • Due to this expertise and position within the company, the contract required his presence in Canada. • The company that he partnered with was a major Canadian company with significant economic output.
Outcome	APPROVED
Analysis	This application was likely approved because a significant amount of time had passed since the commission of the offence and he did not reoffend. Additionally, the applicant demonstrated that he has made a concerted effort to turn his life around by becoming a successful businessperson; indeed, the change from felon to successful businessman is a significant change in circumstances. The specialized nature of his knowledge is highly valuable to a Canadian company and subsequently the Canadian economy, which was likely a major contributing factor to his application's approval.

Client 4

Type of Application	Criminal Rehabilitation and TRP
Offence	1. Disturbing the Peace (*per* Arizona Revised Statutes 13-2904) 2. Assault (*per* Arizona Revised Statutes 13-1203) 3. Damage of Property (*per* Arizona Revised Statutes 13-1602)
Facts	In 1972, the client engaged in a fight and was sentenced to one day in jail. In 1976, while inebriated, he interfered with a DUI arrest and fought with police, damaging the police car and leading to his arrest. He was sentenced to one year probation and a fine. In 1991, he drunkenly forced open the door to the apartment that he shared with his girlfriend. He was placed on one year probation.
Canadian Equivalent	1. s. 175 *Criminal Code*: "Causing a disturbance" 2. s. 129 *Criminal Code*: "Offences relating to public or peace officer", and s. 270: "assault of a peace officer" 3. s. 430 (4) *Criminal Code*: "Mischief"
Reason for Travel	Humanitarian and Compassionate Grounds • Wife is a Canadian citizen whose family lives in Calgary. • Wants to travel to Canada to visit wife's family, specifically her aging father.
Outcome	REFUSED
Analysis	Wife had called the police at least twice in two years to allege that he assaulted her. This was characterized as instability in their domestic relationship and evidence of violent behavior. He was deemed insufficiently rehabilitated, as he didn't express understanding of, or sense of responsibility for, the offences. In fact, the assessing officer called the wife to see if she wanted him in Canada and she said no. Officers have wide discretion to use any information at their disposal when making a determination.

Client 5

Type of Application	TRP
Offence	DUI (per Pennsylvania Code s.3802)
Facts	In December 2007, the client was charged with a DUI and given 5 months probation, 30 days intermediate punishment program (IPP), plus fines and costs. In June 2009 he was charged with a second DUI and charged with 5 months probation, 30 days of electric monitoring, and fines. He completed his second sentence in October 2011.
Canadian Equivalent	s. 253 *Criminal Code*: "Operation while impaired"
Reason for Travel	Humanitarian and Compassionate Grounds • Diagnosed with Stage 3A Hodgkin's Disease, met woman online, with whom he became very close. • He went to visit her and her kids in Ontario, fell in love with her and became father figure to kids. • Wants to marry her. • Later given diagnosis of Non-Hodgkin's Lymphoma, cancer progressed to other parts of his body. • Is receiving experimental RICE treatment. • Still working full-time.
Outcome	APPROVED
Analysis	This client was approved for a TRP because of the strong H&C reasons for travel. It is usually very difficult to obtain a TRP with two recent DUIs on your record. However, the client's situation was considered exceptional enough to warrant special consideration. In many ways, this application exemplifies the purpose of H&C considerations. The client was given only six months to live following his diagnosis (we included a doctor's note that detailed his prognosis); amazingly, he went into remission after spending three months in Canada with his girlfriend. It should be noted that he was also approved for a subsequent TRP.

Client 6

Type of Application	TRP
Offence	Driving while Impaired (New Jersey State Legislature 39:4-50(a))
Facts	In September 2011 the client was driving with his daughter, not wearing proper eyeglasses. He was returning from visiting a friend, and had wine in his system. He was pulled over by a state trooper for an improper lane change. His license was suspended for 3 months.
Canadian Equivalent	s. 253 *Criminal Code*: "Operation while impaired"
Reason for Travel	Leisure and Family • Traveling for Thanksgiving weekend. • Attending an annual high school alumni event in Toronto.
Outcome	DENIED
Analysis	It is uncommon for applicants to be denied TRPs with only one DUI offence on their record. The application was likely denied because so little time had passed between commission of the offence and the application date (the client applied for a TRP in 2013). Additionally, his reasons for travel are not very strong; he would have had a greater likelihood of success if he was traveling for business rather than leisure, or if he had compelling humanitarian reasons (like client 5).

Client 7

Type of Application	Legal Opinion Letter
Offence	Misprision of a felony (per USC s. 4 title 18)
Facts	While president of a gaming company, the client discovered that an officer and director of a competing company were not licensed to distribute certain gaming, but did not report it. He cooperated with the FBI during the rival company's prosecution and was given one-year probation, plus fines. He was granted clemency from the President of the United States and given a full and unconditional pardon.
Canadian Equivalent	There is no real equivalent; closest section is "Not reporting treason" in s. 50 (1)(b) of *Criminal Code*
Outcome	NOT CRIMINALLY INADMISSIBLE
Analysis	The presidential pardon permanently erased all of the charges on his record.

About the Author

Marisa Feil obtained her Bachelor's Degree from McGill University before pursuing her Master's in Common and Civil Law from Université de Montreal, one of Canada's premier law schools. There she completed her thesis on Medical Inadmissibility to Canada and subsequently began her career in Canadian immigration law. After graduation, she started working at one of Canada's largest immigration firms where she noted a lack of comprehensive representation for those wishing to travel to Canada following a criminal conviction.

She consequently started her own firm, Foreign Worker Canada, to address criminal inadmissibility as well as other immigration obstacles. Marisa now guides her clients through the complicated Canadian immigration processes, and assists with the assembly of their applications for entry into Canada. Marisa works with a wide variety of temporary and permanent applications to help her clients live, work, and travel in Canada.

Her practice has succeeded largely in part due to her ability to reach a wide range of clients. Through her open and transparent online presence as well as her outreach and marketing efforts, FWCanada has grown into one of Canada's leading immigration law firms.

Through the strength of her legal counsel and expertise as well as the success of her own firm, Marisa has established herself as a respected authority on matters of Canadian immigration. She is frequently contacted to offer her expertise in lectures, conferences, webinars, and as a contributor in various publications.

When asked at the age of 3 what she wanted to be when she grew up, Marisa Feil calmly responded that she would be a lawyer. Since that day, she has been working toward that goal to become the successful lawyer and entrepreneur that she is today. Marisa is extremely passionate about her work and is motivated by her desire to help others experience life in Canada. She is proud to play an instrumental role in helping people come to Canada who would otherwise be unable to enter.

Index